WHO ARE THE CANTONESE CHINESE?

NEW YORK CITY CHINATOWN DURING THE 1940S-1960S

by

JEAN LAU CHIN

with contributions from

DANIEL LEE

DEDICATION

To our parents: the pioneers who faced the challenges and bore the struggles to enable us to become who we are now.

To the New York City Chinatown community of the 1940s-1960s where we lived these stories; they gave us the impetus and inspiration to our accomplishments today.

This has been an entirely volunteer project through the labor and love of those wanting to preserve and document the history of Cantonese Chinese Americans for future generations. All proceeds from the sale of this book will go to support the work of the New York City Chinatown Oral History Project. Website: www.ceoservices.wix.com/nycchinatownoralhist

CONTENTS

Acknowledgments   i

1   From Rice Fields as Peasant Farmers to Professional Fields as U.S.   1
citizens

2   New York City Chinatown Oral History Project   11

3   Remembrances of Our Times – *Daniel Lee*   16

4   New York City Chinatown   29

5   Community Networks: Shared bonds   42

6   Education: The path to success   59

7   From Laundries and Restaurants to Teachers and Engineers   65

8   Discrimination: Internal and External   70

9   Resiliency   78

10   Extraordinary Accomplishments of Ordinary People—*Jean Lau Chin*   102
and Daniel Lee

11   And we did it in one generation!   113

About the Author   119

ACKNOWLEDGMENTS

Thanks to the many volunteer contributors for the project.

To the Planning Committee, Daniel Lee, Lai Chu, Willie Lau, Eugene Lee, Valerie Tom, Helen Chin, Jim Yuen, Hon Lee, Ann Chan, Pearl Chow, Anna Ong-Shu, Gladys Yan, Gladys Chin, Theodore Ho for their commitment to preserving and documenting our history and untold stories.

To my students, Bernice Chan, Josephine Chuah, Vanessa Li, Kahlen Hong Seon Kim and Lauren Moy who represent the next generation for whom we write these stories.

To all the contributors of the biographies and stories in this book whose experiences and memories are the life of this project—Chinese Americans who grew up in NYC Chinatown during the 1940s-1960s

To the Organization of Chinese Americans-Long Island Chapter for their support of the project

And to the Las Vegas New York Chinatown Reunions where the ideas for this project first germinated.

1 FROM RICE FIELDS AS PEASANT FARMERS TO PROFESSIONAL FIELDS AS U.S. CITIZENS

Who are the Cantonese Chinese?

Lest it be forgotten, the Cantonese Chinese were largely Toisanese—the original Chinese pioneers immigrating to the United States starting in the 1800s for the California Gold Rush. Barred from mining gold because of discrimination, many were recruited as *coolie* laborers building the transcontinental railroad. Immigration grew as the floods in Guangzhou, China from the Yellow River devastated the rice paddies leading to massive starvation and struggles for survival by these peasant farmers.

The Toisanese immigrated to the United States, largely to the seaports of San Francisco in the West, and New York in the East. Because of the restrictive Chinese Exclusion Immigration Laws from 1882 until their repeal in 1943, the Chinese as an ethnic group were specifically barred from entry to the United States. Hence, many entered the United States illegally via *paper names* in search of the *Golden Mountain,* as the United States was called, hoping to striking a fortune and return home to their families. They went on to open laundries and restaurants as the only occupations opened to them. These laws were discriminatory and coupled with intense anti-Chinese sentiment because the Chinese were different and viewed as economic and social threats. The phrase, *"you don't have a Chinaman's chance"* was coined to reflect the reality of an unjust justice system which failed to recognize the basic rights given to white Americans for Chinese Americans.

As the Toisanese Chinese continued to immigrate to the United States, they set up Chinatowns as safe and secure havens where family and community networks gave them a sense of bonding and affiliation and provided the economic supports for their survival. The family clan associations were community social service organizations bonded together by family names; they provided economic support (e.g., loans), housing (e.g., renting out beds), translation services (by the more educated members) as well a community center. Laundry workers living in the outer boroughs generally came to Chinatown once a week on Sundays, their only day off, for groceries and socializing. Chinatowns reinforced the sense of community, and sustained their Chinese identities and cultural values. New York's Chinatown became the second largest Chinatown in the United States next to San Francisco. Following World War II and the forming of the People's Republic of China as a communist country in 1949, immigration of Chinese to the United States was closed.

Chinese Americans remained separated from their families in China for the next two decades. In the meantime, many of these families moved from the Toisan villages to Hong Kong, an urban city colonized by the British made up of primarily Cantonese Chinese. Following President Lyndon Johnson's Family Reunification Act of 1965, many of the Cantonese Chinese from Hong Kong fulfilled their hopes of reuniting with their Toisanese Chinese families in the United States.

Why a book about this group?

Chinese Americans growing up in New York City's Chinatown between the 1940s and 1960s were sandwiched between post-World War II (1941-1945) and the Civil Rights Movement of the 1960s. Anti-Chinese sentiment was rampant as McCarthyism targeted the Chinese as threats to American democracy and our country's security. The world was dichotomized between the free and democratic world of the West allied with the Nationalist Chinese government in Taiwan vs. the communist world with the Soviet Union allied with the People's Republic of China in mainland China. Both claimed to be the legitimate China, and played itself out in NYC Chinatown politics.

The rise and fall of Chinese laundries is a remarkable statement about the struggles and fortitude of the Toisanese Chinese in the U.S. They were replaced by restaurants and garment factory workers as the staple of occupations for Chinese Americans during this time. Most Chinese Americans eked out a living by having two incomes and using child labor in the laundries, restaurants and factories. The "cheap" Chinese food and clothing from the "sweat shops" were a source of exploitation because. restaurant workers were getting subsistence wages relying on tips while garment factory workers received low piecework wages; there were no benefits or job security keeping many families at poverty levels.

What was New York City Chinatown like during the 1940s-1960s? Chinatown was but the five short streets of Mott Street in downtown New York City. The businesses in Chinatown serviced the immigrant Chinese population who spoke little or no English, and had little mobility beyond the confines of Chinatown. Those who came from the outer boroughs of New York City largely owned laundries in neighborhoods where they were the single Chinese family. The children of these Chinese immigrants were largely American born, growing up in an era of Rock and Roll, anti-Chinese discrimination; they were often caught between the traditional values of Chinese culture and the alluring freedom of American democracy.

And yet, the experiences of the Toisanese and now Cantonese Chinese, especially of those from New York City Chinatown, are largely missing from our annals of history. These peasant farmers working the rice fields largely from Toisan, China made extraordinary accomplishments. Their children went on to become responsible U.S. citizens and educated professionals in fields unbeknownst to their parents. As a group, their accomplishments and achievements were unsurpassed. Because there were so few Chinese Americans outside of the laundries and restaurant businesses, their entry into many fields were untraditional and exceptions. They often became the "first". As **Ted Ho**, one of our participants, said: "And we did it in one generation!"

So Why this book about this group of *ordinary people?* Lest it be forgotten, we need to preserve and document these stories, memories, biographies—struggles and accomplishments—of the early Chinese pioneers to the U.S. for the next generations. While the Toisanese were once the majority of the U.S. Chinese American population, they were increasingly replaced by the Cantonese and Taiwanese in the 60s and 70s, then by the Vietnamese Chinese in the 80s, and later by "mainland Chinese" coming largely from Fujian province. This book is not a historical account; rather, it is a psychosocial account of the resiliency, and community networks amidst discrimination and assimilation in a bicultural world—it is written in their voices.

2 NEW YORK CITY CHINATOWN ORAL HISTORY PROJECT

This book is a product of the New York City Chinatown Oral History Project. The project intends to capture the stories and lives of Chinese Americans growing up during the 1940s-1960s in New York City's Chinatown. "Many lived within the 1 mile radius of New York City's Mott Street of Chinatown. Others came from the boroughs, from greater NYC, and from New Jersey for Chinese School or social networking. Today, many have had successful lives and productive careers despite the discrimination and poverty that surrounded us, and the limited opportunities and access to the mainstream. Our Chinese value system and Chinatown community kept us strong....As time moves on, we need to capture the valuable memories and stories of survival and success for our children, ourselves, and for history. Each of us has had some life altering experience; each has had some fond memory that sustained us....We were all ordinary Chinese immigrants; together we made extraordinary strides as a community. We formed the connections, bonds, and support that have lasted a lifetime."(from website: _www.ceoservices.wix.com/nycchinatownoralhist_.

The conviviality of the biennial NYC Chinatown Reunions in Las Vegas since 2000 led many to feel the need to document these stories of a generation that has been forgotten in the annals of U.S. history. We hope the Toisanese will not be forgotten as the original Chinese pioneers to immigrate to the United States beginning in the 1800s. They were the cheap labor contributing to the building of the transcontinental railroad. They were responsible for the introduction of inexpensive tasty Chinese food to the United States in the form of Chow Mein, Chop Suey, Wonton Soup and Egg Rolls catering to western tastes. Although Cantonese food is considered the gourmet of Chinese cuisine in China, this was lost to the many Americans who knew only the above dishes which most Chinese

Americans did not eat.

While there have been many books on Chinese Americans in the U.S, most have been either historical accounts or those originating in the West Coast. The one thing missing in the literature has been the New York City Chinatown story from the East Coast. This is a psychosocial account of the Toisanese and Cantonese Chinese immigrants whose offspring are fondly known as the *Jook Sing generation*. This term was originally coined to be derogatory in characterizing American born Chinese brains as "empty bamboo" because they often spoke no Chinese or knew little of the Chinese culture—it is a form in internal discrimination stemming from Chinese pride of Chinese born immigrants amidst the demeaning existence of laundries and restaurants. The achievements and lived experiences of these first generation American born Chinese are invisible by and large to the American public except through the superficial stereotypes of the "model minority"—quiet, modest, hardworking or in its more demeaning forms of passive, subservient and coolies.

What was it like growing up in America? What was family life in the 40's, 50's, and 60s? What were the community networks? How did they survive the challenges of poverty, discrimination and illegal immigration status? Despite the denial of access to U.S. mainstream resources and opportunities, what are the contributions of this generation? This group is over 60 years old now; most are retired; they care. This book is the first of a series to capture their stories and their accomplishments—in their voices.

The Oral History Project

This book acknowledges all the individuals who have helped to bring this project to fruition. The first group begun in 2008 included: **James Moy, Jim Yuen, Gladys Chin, Daniel Lee** asking their peers to contribute their stories. As **Jim Yuen**, a now retired IT manager, said, many Chinese are private, and were reluctant to make themselves known in contributing to the stories and pictures hosted on his website, *Memories of NYC Chinatown*, (http://chinatown.aditl.com). Pictures from the Las Vegas reunions date back to 2002 though he never attended a single reunion. **James Moy,** a minister with a PhD in psychology, made the early attempts to inspire those to write and record their stories. **Daniel Lee,** a licensed professional engineer, was the persistent one to share stories and memories, write chronologies and facts about Chinatown in the 1930s, 40s, 50s, and 60s; he circulated these via email as yet another way to urge people to participate. He too has never attended a reunion, but maintains contact with scores of friends from this era. Many of his emails records conversations of fond memories and inspirational stories about growing up during this era which are included in this book. **Gladys Chin**, one of the founders and organizer of the biennial Las Vegas NYC Chinatown reunions for many years, circulated the many stories she received and published them in the reunion booklets. As she says, "I did not live or grow up in Chinatown; I grew up in Newark, NJ, but married someone from Chinatown".

This effort, begun in 2002, faltered as many , though enthusiastic about the project, simply did not contribute stories—life intervened with retirement, grandchildren, health, etc. Or perhaps they simply fit the Asian stereotype of: not wanting to toot our own horns. A second group, begun in 2010 without knowledge of this prior effort, included: **Lai Chu, Hon Lee, Eugene Lee, Willie Lau, and Jean Lau Chin**. Their bios are included in the stories throughout book. Foremost in the minds of both groups was the wish to capture and preserve these stories *for our children and next generations* as identified in the foreword. Equally important was the wish to establish the legacy of the Toisanese Chinese as the early pioneers of Chinese in America.

The two groups soon joined efforts. We met with a continued reluctance to contribute stories despite the huge enthusiasm for the project.—whether it was time or modesty. We then hosted a *50s Party* in New York City to kick off the project once again. Making use of the group comradery and wish to come together, this event brought together over 140 people. We recorded stories and memories in small groups using a structured set of questions asking participants to talk about their fondest memories and the challenges of growing up. **Corky Lee**, fondly known as the *undisputed unofficial Asian American Photographer Laureate* came to take group pictures. Many brought memoirs along to share. A new phase in the project began with the volunteer efforts of my graduate students in psychology to assist in recording interviews with the seniors for their stories.

The project now included an intergenerational dimension as my young adult Asian American students interviewed seniors who were the age of their parents and grandparents. While contributing to the project, they gained new insights into their own family histories from these experiences. **Bernice Chan**, one of the interviewers who was born in NYC but attending school at Wellesley College in Massachusetts, said, "I got a lot out of the project in the last six weeks and loved listening and recording the stories. I learned so much of my own Toisanese history and people. Talking about the project with my family actually sparked conversations about their own pasts and memories of Chinatown and being Chinese American, which were things we had hardly ever talked about."

This began a series of individual interviews for those unwilling or unable to write their own stories. It captured the richness of narratives that were reminiscent, inspiring, and documentary. But as **Lily Ho and Dottie Chin** both commented, "We should be talking about our parents' stories. Their struggles and their challenges are what enabled us to reach the achievements we did. Their stories should not be forgotten." This will become the project's next phase. This book is the first of several installations to come.

Individual Bio Sketches and Stories

Included in this Who's Who book are the bio sketches and stories which are embellished with the psychosocial contexts of the times. The selected bios with photographs of the participants give a face and voice to the stories, and commemorates our participants. They are voluntary contributions of individual Chinese Americans who grew up in NYC Chinatown during the 1940s-1960s. They vary from simple paragraphs or quotes to more detailed stories and themes. Space does not permit the full interviews to be published. We apologize for these omissions, and regret our inability to include all the stories we received for this volume.

Some stories are unique; others are such common experiences among many of the participants that they are *everyone's story*. The fathers of these mostly American born Chinese were largely restaurant workers or laundry owners while the mothers were largely garment factory seamstresses or did piecework beading. Most of the families came from modest backgrounds. Most were from the small villages in Toisan, in the southern province of Guangzhou China. The remaining were from Sun Voy, Jung Sun, Hoy Ping or Hakka—all neighboring districts of Toisan except for the Hakka who were considered the wanderers. As shown on the map, the Toisan district was miniscule within the Guangzhou province and even more so within the vastness of China. And yet, they accounted for almost all of the early immigrants responsible for building the transcontinental railroad, and recruited as *coolie labor* during the California Gold Rush.

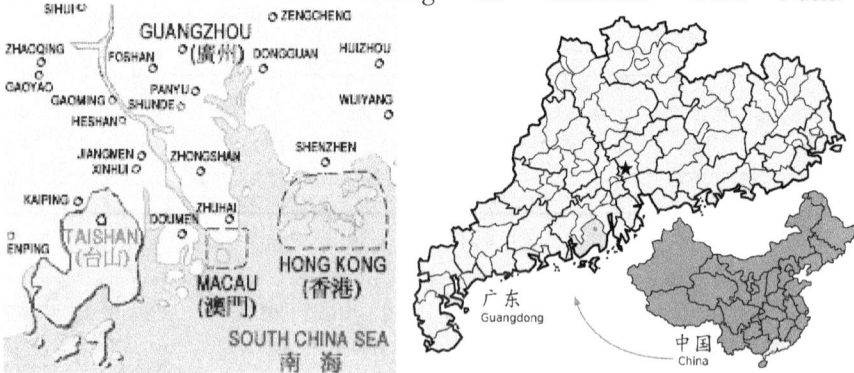

The 1882 Project

Most of these families were directly impacted by the Chinese Exclusion laws of 1882 preventing the entry of Chinese to the U.S. Many resorted to illegal entry to the U.S. up until 1965 when President Lyndon Johnson's Executive Order 11246 led to the reunification of families.

Since 2010 the 1882 Project, a non-partisan coalition Chinese Americans nationwide, together with Asian American leaders and supporters, pushed for a formal apology from Congress for enacting a series of Chinese Exclusion laws prohibiting people of Chinese ancestry from becoming naturalized citizens in the U.S. from 1882 to 1943.

With the passage of Senate Resolution 201 (Oct. 2011) and House Resolution 683 (June 2012), the 112th Congress provided a formal apology. This is the fifth time ever that Congress has made such an apology to a group of people, and took almost 130 years. The 1882 Project led by Michael Lin from OCA-APAA helped to raise public awareness of how influential, pervasive and discriminatory these laws were to the Chinese.

Despite the Accomplishments, the Fear Continues

The collection of stories in this book present almost a uniform story of the shared life experiences of Chinese Americans growing up in NYC Chinatown during the 1940s-60s. The accomplishments are many of individuals as they forged careers and lives that their parents only aspired to in their dreams. Many served in the U.S. military and fought in the Korean or Vietnam War. The parents were the pioneers whose sole goal and many sacrifices were to make a better life for their children in immigrating to the United States. They would be proud to see these biographies. And yet, despite these accomplishments, many of these American born Chinese U.S. citizens continue to harbor a fear that U.S. sentiment might reverse one day to threaten their security and safety in the U.S. They speak in cautious tones about their paper names.

3 REMEMBRANCES OF OUR TIMES – *DANIEL LEE*

These remembrances chronicle world and local events during the 1940s-1960s, setting the context for many of the stories told by the contributors in this book. It is followed by the social and community activities and landmarks in NYC Chinatown which are frequently referenced and experienced by the contributors.

Chronology....

Memorable Moments and Unforgettable Narratives on the Chinatown Happenings and World Events of that Era When We Were Growing Up.....Highlights and Essences of the late 1940's , 1950's, and early 1960's!

1948–Cornerstone laid for True Light Lutheran Church; Polaroid Camera Introduced; Subway Ride—Five Cents; Chinese Intercity Basketball Tournaments begin; the first 33 1/3 rpm LP is sold.

1949–Bikini Swimsuits are the Fad; NY Yankees Defeat Brooklyn Dodgers to Win World Series; The first 45 rpm Records is sold; China becomes a Communist Country under Mao Tse-Tung.

1950 –Price of Average Home--$8500.00; NYC has Severe Water Shortage--prolong drought; USAF Academy opens in Colorado Springs CO; US population at 151 Million; Korean War starts.

1951–Color TV is introduced; Minimum Wage is 75 Cents/Hour; Rock and Roll is the new musical rage—Alan Freed; Baked Char Sui Bow becomes the latest hit on Bayard St at Lin Heung Coffee Shoppe.

1952—Dr. Salk discovers Polio Vaccine; Average Annual Salary is $4500.00; Dr. Lee's- Best Shoeshine—10 Cents on Mott St; American Bandstand makes its debut with Dick Clark; US develops the first Hydrogen Bomb.

1953–IBM releases the first Computer; Playboy Magazine arrives; Bowl of "Just Wonton Soup" is 35 cents; Chinatown Baseball Team in Ice Cream League; **Lonnie's Coffee Shoppe Opens at 21 Mott St..**

1954—Postage Stamp is 3 Cents; First McDonald's opens; TV Dinners debut; USS Nautilus is the first Atomic Submarine; Latin dancing, the

Mambo, Cha Cha, and Merengue are the latest Hot Sizzling Dances.

1955—DA Haircuts are the Fad; Third Ave El demolished; Disneyland opens in California.

1956—Elvis Presley debuts on Ed Sullivan Show; A Car Costs $2,100.00; Dow Jones at 500; NY Yankee Don Larsen pitches first No Hitter in World Series; **Miss Chinatown NY-Debbie Gong.**

1957---Ford debuts the Edsel—a failure; both NY baseball teams play their last game—Brooklyn Dodgers at Ebbets Field and NY Giants at Polo Grounds; Russia launches Sputnik into Earth's Orbit.

1958—Hula Hoop Craze begins; Harvard tuition at $1200.00; Stereo sound introduced to Hi-Fi Fans; NASA created for the Space Age; US launches Explorer 1; first Japanese cars, Toyotas and Datsuns, are imported to US.

1959—Debut of compact cars—Corvair and Falcon; Mattel debuts Barbie Doll; Gas is 25 cents a gallon; Movie tickets are $1.00; Boeing 707 Jetliner comes into service; Alaska becomes the 49th state; Hawaii becomes the 50th state of the US.

1960—Chubby Checker introduces *The Twist* and becomes the craze; the play Fantasticks opens in Greenwich Village and starts a 42 year run; US Population at 180 million; first Playboy Club opens in Chicago.

1961—NY Yankee Roger Maris hits record setting 61 Home Runs; China's Population at 650 million; Berlin Wall separates East and West Germany; Peace Corps created by President John F. Kennedy.

1962—American Astronaut John Glenn orbits Earth 3 Times; Cuban Missile Crisis; Diet Coke introduced; Bosa Nova and Watusi becomes the latest dance craze; Playboy Club opens in NYC.

1963—Average Worker earns over $100.00 a week; ATT introduces Touch Tone phone; Dr. Martin Luther King Jr. makes his*I Have a Dream Speech*; President Kennedy is assassinated in Dallas, Texas.

1964---Discotheques and Go-Go Dancing in a cage makes its debut; England's Beetles make TV debut on Ed Sullivan Show; World's Fair in Flushing Meadows NY in 1964 and 1965; US becomes heavily involved in Vietnam War.

1965---NYC has massive blackout; latest fashion are Bell Bottom Trousers and Mini Skirts; flip top cans for Soft Drinks and Beer introduced; US Congress pass Immigration Act of 1965.

Chinatown as a Center of Activity....

Chinatown provided the **family and social connected infrastructure** for Chinese in the greater NY Metropolitan area as witnessed by the *busy family activities* on Sundays' in the shops and family associations. Banquets on successive Sundays were frequent following the Chinese Lunar New Year celebrations and festivities in the 40's, 50's, and 60's. For young Chinese adults looking for a social setting and meeting new people, NYC's Chinatown was a *magnet* for **socials** and **sports** activities for children and young adults from the NY metropolitan area; Boston, MA; Philadelphia, PA; Washington, DC; and Newark, NJ right across the Hudson River and

as far away as Toronto and Montreal, Canada. As a result, many relationships developed during these **socials** and **sports** events with *dating, couples going steady, long lasting friendships,* and *marriages* among these young adults from the Chinatown community.

Settling in the New York/New Jersey Metropolitan Area....

Upon reminiscing back on our life in Chinatown, several questions that come to mind are: What were the **events and circumstances** that led our grandparents, parents, and families to settle in America and New York's Chinatown? What was the **intriguing genealogy** of why so many of the **"Eng family lineage"** settled in *Newark NJ* and the surrounding NJ towns rather than Chinatown? Did our ancestors and families go through **Angel Island** in California or **Ellis Island** in New York for immigration processing? Why did the **Mandarin Chinese** settle uptown?

Chinatown in the 1940's and 1950's....

NYC's Chinatown then had a border on the Bowery from Canal Street. to Chatham Square wrapping around Worth and Mulberry Streets back to Canal St. (At one time, the 3rd Ave El rumbled above the streets on the Bowery to Chatham Square

before turning into Park Row to go down to City Hall or to South Ferry; *bums* and the homeless were known to hang out under the El.). The streets in Chinatown were Mott, Pell, Doyers, Park, Bayard, and Elizabeth Streets. On the peripheral of Chinatown were Forsyth, Chrystie, Division, Henry, East Broadway, Madison, Catherine, Oliver Street(s) and St. James Place

Overcoming Negative Stereotyping.......

In the Chinatown community, we had strong family values and close loving parents; a proactive family emphasis on education; proper church teaching and guidance; and good school teachers who helped frame our academic foundation and discipline for later educational, social, economic, and professional achievements. From our perspective, the negative American connotation of the Chinese laundryman, laborer, houseboy, Charlie-the waiter, etc. were all but eradicated in one generation by the successes and accomplishments made by the young adults who grew up in Chinatown and the surrounding metropolitan areas

Exceptional Generation of Kids.......

When we look back at our life in Chinatown and the greater surrounding NY Metropolitan area, our generation had a high percentage of smart, talented, and resourceful kids who were self-motivated and driven through education and hard work to succeed in life. Our *small* Chinatown community produced a *large* number of success stories with our share of entrepreneurs, businessmen, and professionals. The results are a positive indicator of our many blessings and how we successfully managed life's challenges to be the *"best you can be in life"*

Discrimination........

We became aware of discrimination against Chinese Americans outside Chinatown, especially when we were in high school, worked in Chinese restaurants on weekends and the summers where we met waiters in their 30's to 40's, who were college graduates from schools like Columbia, New York University, and City College of New York. They had experienced difficulties getting jobs after graduation while their white classmates readily received job offers. In order to sustain themselves and their families, they started working in the restaurant business. After a few years of unsuccessfully trying to get jobs in their fields of study, one can appreciate the difficulties of trying to get higher level jobs when one's resume shows recent work experience as being a waiter or a bartender. However, a number of these industrious waiters and bartenders went on to start their own businesses and in the long run were probably better off financially in the business world......must be that *true Chinese entrepreneurial DNA in the blood*.

Small Minority with Many Significant Contributions.........

Although Chinese Americans are classified as a minority group, we have made *significant contributions* in the sciences, engineering, technology, medicine, finance, education, and businesses contributing to the *intellectual, cultural, and material wealth of America*. It may be another generation before the population size increases to a level where there will be a higher representation of Chinese Americans/Asian Americans in political circles to have a significant impact and become a major forceful influence on the policies of both political parties and the direction of this country. That day will indeed be the *tipping point* where Chinese Americans/ Asian Americans will be **a** *dynamic influential political force*

Chinatown Teen Socials...........

The **"Teen Hops"** were held at the Transfiguration Catholic Church and Mariners Temple where many of the Chinatown teenagers were able to meet and socialize with teenagers from the other New York boroughs and New Jersey.

Chinatown Social Life.........

On the "**social scale**", there was the **Ging Hawk Club** in the early 50's followed by the **Four Seas Club** on 22 Pell Street; the **Jade Club** on 20 E. Broadway; and other smaller social clubs in the late 50's and the 60's. The **Jaycees** hosted the annual New Year's Eve Dance Party in the early 60's at the Commodore Hotel and in subsequent years at the St. George Hotel in Brooklyn, NY. Many of the larger dances were held at the Mac Burney YMCA on 23rd St. and major NYC hotels; college dances sponsored by the respective Chinese Student Societies were held at the City College(s), Columbia, and NYU; and church socials were held after basketball games at True Light Church (True Light boys' and girls' basketball teams "Daughters of China" (DOC) and Mariners Temple.

Bear Mountain Summer Family-Social Excursion........

During the summer, everyone looked forward to the last Monday in July when the *Chinese American Restaurant Association* held its **"annual boat ride"** from **South Ferry** to **Bear Mountain** starting at 8:00 am and returning at 11:00 pm. Here was an opportunity to see old friends and meet new ones as there were all kinds of activities for people of all ages and it was truly a family outing with something for everyone to participate in from various games of chance; to dancing; to a table tennis contest; to a dance contest; to a food festival of great home cooked food; to just plain socializing and meeting new people on the boat; to a picnic and swimming at Bear Mountain; and to the return trip under moon light and dancing away the night were memories to remember and cherish.

Sports, Recreation, and Relaxation.......

For various sports and ball games, there were Columbus Park, Bridge Park, and Forsyth Park; and the gyms at the Church of All Nations, True Light Lutheran Church, Transfiguration Catholic Church, and Mariners Temple. Teams like the *Clowns, Mohawks, Cathy, Pirates, and Bengals* competed in basketball tournaments. True Light Church had a basketball team that competed with other Lutheran Churches in a Protestant Church League. For a little recreation and relaxation during the summer, there was **Coney**

Island with the world famous *Cyclone* and *Parachute* rides with swimming at the *Washington Baths* (*Salt Water Pool*) and *Nathan's hot dogs*. When we were able to drive, **Jones Beach** was the place to be with the white sand beaches and we concluded the day with a quiet beach party at night under the stars on the sand dunes. Many Chinatown families had homes or rentals in **Bradley Beach NJ** and *"Newark Ave."* became *"Chinatown"* on the Jersey Shore during the summer months.

Annual Baby Contest—Columbus Park......

Another annual event worth remembering was the **"Baby Contest"** held at Columbus Park as part of the annual **Chinese Community Club's** (CCC) **Field Day** with games, refreshments, and socializing followed by a serious softball game with a team from Philadelphia's Chinatown. Some may remember being crowned *King* or *Queen* for the day or being the first or second runner-up at the Baby Contest.

Recreational Weekend Retreats......

Throughout the year, there were many other social activities like the

Chinese Christian Youth Conference (CCYC) and **China Institute** which had summer and winter social/sport/church related long weekend retreats to Pawling NY, Lake George NY, and the Berkshires in Pittsfield MA. Other groups like the **Long Island Chinese Circle** had their social functions for many of the people who had moved out to Long Island.

Double Ten Celebration and Beauty Pageant......

In addition to **Chinese Lunar New Year,** which was usually celebrated in January or February depending on the lunar calendar, the other big Chinese holiday in Chinatown was the *Chinese Independence Day* (Sun Yat Sen's declaration of independence from the former emperor rule) celebrated on *October 10th* or commonly known as **Double Ten.** Under the direction of progressive minded organizers in the mid 50's, the Chinatown Merchant's Association initiate and organized the **Miss Chinatown New York Contest** and to celebrate the **Double Ten** holiday. A grand parade consisting of association sponsored imaginative parade floats carrying beautiful contestants; Chinese School and True Light Marching Bands; Lion Dances from the associations; community dignitaries including politicians

and veterans' organizations marched their way through the narrow and winding streets of Chinatown. Miss Debbie Gong from Queens, NY was crowned "Miss Chinatown New York" in 1956.

Since **Latin American dancing** was the hot tempo *in craze* at the time, a decision was made by the Chinatown planning committee to have a dance contest in **Mambo, Cha Cha, Merengue, Rumba**, and **Samba** with a judging panel led by "Killer" Joe Pirro from the world famous **Palladium on Broadway.** *Danny Lee* from Chinatown and *Carol Lee* (Chinese-Cuban) from Cuba were fortunate and privileged to be the winning couple of these five Latin American Dance Contest competitions, as part of the **"Double Ten"** celebration festivities

PS 23 Public School K—6ᵗʰ Grades........

From **Public School, PS 23** on the corner of *Mulberry and Bayard Streets*, there were the teachers: Mrs. Reardon, third grade; Miss Connelly, fourth grade; Mrs. Gellis, fifth grade; and Mrs. Brown (Miss Carbone) sixth grade.

Mrs. Brown was an exceptional teacher and disciplinarian who taught us all the fundamentals in math and English to prepare us for junior and senior high. For the kids living on the peripheral streets of Chinatown, there was **PS 1** for grades K—6ᵀᴴ on Henry & Catherine Streets.

PS 130 Public School 7ᵗʰ and 8ᵗʰ Grades......

Next in the educational line was the ***physical combat zone*** of **PS 130** for seventh and eighth grades on the corner of *Hester and Baxter Streets* in **Little Italy**. It certainly was a diversified and engaging two year experience and *explicit exposure to racial discrimination.* At PS 130, Chinese were the minority whereas; we had been the majority at PS 23. It was certainly a different set of experiences and ***life lessons learned*** about discrimination in true living color compared to the ***safe*** PS 23 environment in Chinatown. For the kids living on the peripheral streets of Chinatown, there was **JHS 65** for the seventh, eighth and ninth grades on Forsyth Street.

Chinese Schools........

Then there was the old Wah Keuh Chinese School on Mott St after going to American School all day. Many of us went to the old Chinese School before it was torn down and rebuilt as a community center and Chinese School. Parochial school was available at the Transfiguration Catholic Church which had both American and Chinese Schools.

Active Mix of Chinatown Academic and Social Life........

During the high school and college years of the late 40's, 50's and early 60's, it was not just all work and school studies with no play. For many, there were social functions to attend on any given weekend such as private parties; dances sponsored by various club(s) or group(s); college parties or dances; and church socials held after basketball games; or one could just play stick ball, shoot pocket pool or billiards with the guys or go bowling with your friends.

Tales of 37 Mott, 44 Mulberry Street, and 47 Mott Street......

There were the larger buildings like 37 Mott and 44 Mulberry which was another community hub. **37 Mott** is located in the center of Chinatown at the crossroads of Mott and Pell Street. It is like a little village within Chinatown where you probably knew some of the families even if you didn't live there. **44 Mulberry** is right across the street from Columbus Park where the residents can appreciate the grass and trees in the park. Both buildings had many families and tons of untold stories and interesting tales to recall and tell.

47 Mott has a distinction all of its own since five medical doctors, a few Ph.D.'s, and engineers came from this building. What were the secrets to these academic and professional success stories?

Chinatown Canal St. Subway Station Conveniences to Entertainment and Shopping......

From Chinatown, one can easily take the BMT subway to **42rd St. and Times Square** to see a movie at any number of theaters on the *"Great White Way"* or to take in a movie or stage show at the Roxy or Radio City Hall. On **34th St. and Herald Square** and **14th St. and Union Square**, one can shop at top department stores like Macys and Gimbels. All these activities are within one to three express stops from the Canal Street subway station. One can even go over to DeKalb Ave in **downtown**

Brooklyn which was one subway stop away to see a movie at the Paramount, Fox, or Albee Theaters. Fulton Street was also well known for great shopping in department stores like A&S, Loesers, and Namns.

Bowling as a Popular Activity...........

For the bowlers, there were the **Roxy, Mid City, and City Hall Bowling Alleys** to choose from and to find out where the real financial competition was taking place for the weekend. Some of us even went roller-skating at the **Gay Blades Roller Rink** a few blocks from the Roxy.

Chinatown Fair.......

A little penny arcade and play land which had a gift shop, skee ball with prizes, and a juke box was located under the famous Port Arthur Restaurant. Children and tourists alike would enjoy themselves inside from the busy activities outside on Mott Street. It was not Coney Island or Palisades Park penny arcades, but enough fun and laughs for the Chinatown children and tourists passing through, especially the dancing chicken...

Chinatown Post Office and Buddhist Temple.......

A US Post Office also known as the *"world's smallest"* right in the heart of Chinatown where the packages overflowed on to the front sidewalk during the Christmas holiday season. The people waiting to get into the post office and the tourists waiting to visit the *Buddhist Temple* in the back of the building all standing side by side on the sidewalk was a sight to remember.

Chinatown Pharmacy......

The Chinatown Pharmacy on 47 Mott Street was the first Chinese owned western style pharmacy in New York City. Besides serving as a local drug store, it was also a meeting place, message center, and social hangout. The pharmacy working with the Chinese Community Club (CCC) sponsored a number of community events like Christmas parties for Chinatown children, athletic teams, Spring Field Day and Baby Parade, Chinese New Year Ballroom Dance, and a Chinese New Year Lion Dance troop.

Post-Midnight--Little Snack... Noodles and Rice..."Seow Yeah"

After a long day, a party, a dance, a movie, a date, or quality time with

friends, *Seow Yeah* (meaning little somethings) sounds like a delightful snack before retiring. This little snack could be an order of noodles on a platter with your choice of meat or seafood and vegetable cooked with your favorite sauce. Noodles can also be served in a soup with your favorite selection of ingredients to your taste. Rice dishes are steaming rice on a platter with your selected topping of meat, seafood, & vegetable in a sauce of your choice. There are a *large variety of menu selections written only in Chinese and posted on the wall* at Chinatown restaurants that specialize in this type of service. Popular among the noodle houses for "Seow Yeah" are Hong Fat, Sam Wo, and Wo Hop on Mott St.; New Lin Heung on Bayard St.; and Hop Kee on Doyers St. **When did we ever sleep?**

Yum Cha—"Dim Sum".....A Cantonese Delight......

Remember the casual bakery and tea houses like Nom Wah on Doyers St. and Tung Kee on Chatham Square serving *Dim Sum*—Sui Mai, Har Gow, Shrimp or Beef Cheung Foon, Char Sui and Steam Pork Bows, Egg Tarts. and many other tasty pastries? Meanwhile, the more formal lunch time *Yum Cha* (drinking tea) and *Dim Sum* were served at restaurants like Lee's, Pagoda, and Port Arthur. As *Dim Sum* grew in popularity, many smaller

coffee shops and bakeries became innovative and served yummy *Dim Sum* and other savory specialties at competitive prices for us to enjoy. What other ethnic or world cuisine can be sampled from such a large variety of delicious *Dim Sum* dishes and pastries at such reasonable prices? The wonders of **"Dim Sum"** literally means **"point to the heart's desire"—a** *gourmet's delight indeed...*

Lonnie's Coffee Shop.......

An *instant success* and a convenient meeting place for the high school, college, and young adult age groups to hang out and enjoy American food on the corner of Mott and Park Street. The menu was simple and *different* with hamburgers, sandwiches, juices, sodas, ice cream, pastries, and coffee.

Anyone interested in a **Lime Rickey** or **Egg Cream** with NYC's one and only world famous **Sutter's Pastries**? *Just yummy and a little tease…..for* **the sweet tooth in us….**

Final Thoughts and a Request……

My thoughts and remembrances of the Chinatown happenings and events of the 40's, 50's, and 60's periods of our youth are offered as part of my experiences seen through my prism. As we continue on our adventure and journey through life, let us be grateful to the ones who led the way for us in the 30's and early 40's by ***celebrating the past*** and for their many sacrifices and contributions. Do ***enjoy the present***, *every moment of it*, and continue ***believing in the future*** to preserve the past for our children and grandchildren, to serve as a role model for them, to be inspired by how we, through a good education, overcame many challenges; learned a lot with hard work; had a fun time in the process; and maintained our strong family and religious values to succeed in life.—*Daniel Lee*

4 NEW YORK CITY CHINATOWN

Growing up in Chinatown

There are those who lived and grew up in NYC Chinatown. Their daily lives were surrounded by other Chinese within a community only 3 blocks long and two blocks wide. Those living on the Lower East Side, less than a mile away, did not feel they "lived" in Chinatown. Today, NYC Chinatown is one of the largest in the country, and has taken over what had been Little Italy on Mulberry Street, crossing over Canal Street and the Bowery.

Chinatown was their community. And "it was safe until we crossed Canal Street into the Italian neighborhood". Extended family members came forth to support one another—for employment, for social life, for economic support, and as surrogate parents for children without their parents.

Those living in Chinatown largely recall the *cold water flats* in railroad type apartments. There was no hot water, no toilets in the apartment; bathtubs were in the kitchen. Communal toilets were in the hall, and apartments were walk-up without elevators. Families of 5 or more often lived in 3 room apartments where children shared one bedroom and the living room often doubled as sleeping quarters. Many recall such things as: the kerosene stoves used for heating, the blocks of ice for the *icebox*, and the absence of TV and air conditioning. Most were poor, but "never knew it" because "everyone else faced the same struggles" or "managed to get by" with the help of extended family. Children created their own games of stick ball (with broom sticks as bats), derby carts (made out of milk crates), even climbing the rooftops of Chinatown—all ingenious inventions by those of limited resources, and urban living.

Then there were those who came from the outer boroughs of Queens, Brooklyn, and the Bronx, and even parts of New Jersey to Chinatown. As young children, their families came to Chinatown on Sundays, their only day off. They came for grocery shopping, for socializing, and for business. It was their community too as most were *the lone Asians* in the neighborhoods where they lived and owned laundries or restaurants. The teens came for their social life—to the churches (True Light and Transfiguration), to the dances sponsored by the clubs, or to just hang out. Many came for the Wah Keuh Chinese School, 5 days a week in addition to regular American school, often traveling more than one hour by public transportation to get there. It was not uncommon for children as young as 6 to be accompanied by older siblings because their parents were working. Family and community values of education, hard work, resiliency, and "having face" permeated through parental messages and extended family behaviors.

John Mok: *Living in Chinatown, we didn't know we were Chinese.* Everything was Chinese.

Lived at: 34 Mott Street, Chinatown
Now living in: New Jersey
Born: 1942
Occupation: Accounting, worked for General Electric and then AT&T
Father's Occupation: Laundry
Mother's Occupation: one of the first teachers in P.S. 23
Unique experience: My grandfather, Lee Bee Lok, came to this country in 1895, and opened Quong Yuen Shing, which came to be known at the *Chinese Post Office* (see story by Clifford Lee). My grandfather had 6 girls and one son; his goal was to put all those girls and son through college, and get an education. (He was ahead of his times in valuing education for his daughters as well as his son). My mother was employed by the Bank of China on Wall Street; that was pretty prestigious at the time instead of working in the laundry or restaurant. Then my mother became one of the first Chinese Americans to become a NYC school teacher; she taught at P.S. 23 from about 1950 to 1975 when she was in her 40s, also having attended there. My father came to the U.S. in 1923 for college. Upon graduation, he opened a laundry in Freeport, Long Island because there were no available job opportunities.

We had a wonderful childhood; my grandfather ended up buying a house in Bradley Beach, NJ as did many Chinese from Chinatown also did; it cost $2000 at that time. Growing up with both parents who were college educated as well my aunts and one uncle was quite atypical at the time. I was one of 7 Chinese American students at Stuyvesant; most of the students were Jewish at the time. Living in Chinatown, we didn't know we were Chinese because everyone was. Then you crossed Canal Street going to JHS at PS 130 was like "Wow! You better get back home fast after 3PM.

I don't know very much about my family background; while my mother was very open, she was also the oldest one so she would not divulge a lot of things. She had to take care of her father and mother when they were ill—but like many Chinese would say, "you don't talk about those things!" They were not old-fashioned, it's just the way they were raised. When you asked your parents things like, "why do we do this?, why can't we wear black", we were told, "That's the way it is." There was always a preference for the color red. We never talked about death, illness, and sickness—the dark side of life. My father was more modern than my mother even though she was American born. He loved this country. He never went home (to China) after immigrating here. I've always found that strange that they didn't speak Chinese to us although they spoke to each other in Chinese. But when I would go down to my grandfather's store, they would all speak Chinese.

William Lee: *Chinatown was safe until you crossed over Canal St.*

Nickname: Kok Doy
Lived in: 37 Mott Street, Chinatown
Now living at: Yorktown Heights, NY
Born: 1941

Fondest Memory: Chinatown was safe. It was our territory. Everyone knew one another. It was safe until we crossed over Canal St to Little Italy and would get beaten up by the Italian kids. My fondest memory is how we used to take the Staten Island Ferry for 5 cents to go across and come back.

Ann Chan: *I was given up for adoption because my family was too poor*

Born: 1930s in the Bronx
Lived at: Chinatown
Father's Occupation: Laundry

Mother's Occupation: garment factory and beading

Biography: I found out at age 15 that I was given up for adoption when I was one month old because my family had 8 children, 6 daughters, and was too poor. My adopted mother gave my biological mother a *hung bow* (red envelope) of $25 for me. I married young at age 18, but it was a marriage that lasted more than 50 years.

When my adopted mother went to Hong Kong for my grandmother's 75th birthday; she died of a brain hemorrhage on the way there. My adopted father was a Chinese interpreter for the On Leong clan association (Chinese Merchants Association) where he used to bail people out after they were arrested for gambling. After my mother's death, my father was so distraught he started drinking, and died soon after. I then raised my

brother who was only 15 at the time. Despite limited resources, I managed to pay for his wedding when he was in his 20s.

Unique experience: We were among the first to move out from Chinatown to Long Island. Together, a group of women, largely Hunter College graduate, formed the Ging Hawk Club in the 1940s; this was one of the first Chinese civic groups on Long Island. This group later became the Long Island Circle, which is now the Chinese Cultural Institute of Long Island, offering Chinese School, traditional Chinese dancing for the suburban Chinese. I helped to raise money, sponsor programs, and bring in local politicians to promote the visibility of our community.

(Ann's story of adoption was typical of the mindset among many in the Chinese community at the time which devalued girls and struggled with poverty. The tragic death of her adoptive parents compounded her sense of loss. However, her resiliency is evident in her raising her young brother and going on to be an active leader in the Chinese American community. Despite facing much discrimination in her own career, her motivation to give back to the community and help the underdog led her to become one of the forerunners of Chinese social and community service on Long Island. She has helped to develop many social and civic programs for families and seniors.)

Ivan Chin: Don't let people look down on you

Born: 1941
Lived at: 59 Bayard St, Chinatown
Occupation: Restaurant
Father's occupation: died when he was age 3
Mother's occupation: seamstress in garment factory
Biography: We were latch key kids because our parents were always working. When my mother was widowed, the community stepped in to help the family. Relatives from our village in China would watch over me. I did not experience discrimination growing up in Chinatown because we were all struggling. Our Chinese values included: respect, hard work and maintaining face. My mother always told us: "Don't let people look down on you (Mo ay yan hi sleu)." (The importance of "having face" no matter the circumstances was stressed by many.)

We played basketball a lot and *stoop ball* on the steps. We'd go to the hardware store to buy a broom stick, get it cut, and play stickball by the court house. Gitkie, Eugene, Bobby, and the 37 group would play in the park and at True Light Church. We were the *Chumps* for the Crusades. None of our courts were regulation size compared to when we played with the Caucasians. I also belonged to the Boy Scouts. When we went to *PS* 130 for junior high school, we used have a lot fights because we were bullied by the Italians.

Wah Keuh Chinese School was a forced thing; we had to go. If we spoke English at home, my mother would feel we were talking about her so we spoke Chinese. We had nicknames for the Chinese School teachers; there was *stiff neck*, the *black widow* because she had no husband. They were strict; one day, I was playing with my Mickey Mouse watch and Woo Seen Sang (teacher)took it from me; I never got it back.

Irene Kwong: Moving on Up to Queens

Born: 1947
Lived at: Henry St, Chinatown
Now living in: New Hyde Park
Biography: I came to America at age 5. Wanting a
better education, my father transferred me to
Transfiguration for high school. I graduated with
honors, and was fortunate to get free public college
education at City College. This enabled me to work
in corporate America. Otherwise, I would have
ended up like my mother working in the garment
factories sewing. Education turned my life around.
I was very lucky. I could have been a high school
dropout.

I lost a lot [of my culture] because I wanted so
hard to assimilate in America; I don't know if that's a good or bad thing.
Unlike this generation where you are proud of your heritage; then, everyone
wanted to be American. Wanting a better life, we moved out to Queens
when I was 15 years old from a 2 room flat in Chinatown. That was all we
knew until we moved to Queens. Then you realize, "Oh my god, this is
how the rest of the world lives". We moved to Jackson Heights into a 2
family house; I had my own bedroom, living room, driveway; but there
weren't any Chinese out there then.

And others

Leilani Chin: born in NYC Chinatown. My family
did not come from Toisan. My father was an actor
for the Hong Kong Chinese Opera; He met my
mother in Hawaii. They came in 1940 for 1 year
when the WWII broke out; they stayed in the US.
My brother and I were born here.
Fondest Memories: My
fondest memories are of being
backstage of Sun Sing Theatre
where my father performed. I would watch the
women change into their costumes before the
Operas. I was in the shows when they needed
children. I didn't come to Chinatown until my older
sister came here from China.

Helen Chin: I used to be a Lau; I grew up in the
outskirts of Chinatown. My first experience with
Chinatown was when I went to Transfiguration

Church and met a lot of Chinese people with whom I could relate. My parents were friends with Anna and Jeannie. When they visited, we would take walks to Chinatown.

Chinatown Businesses

For some of those in Chinatown, their parents were the owners of the businesses that sustained the community. These businesses provided everything from groceries and restaurants to insurance and legal services. The food in Chinatown was "authentic", unlike the fortune cookies, egg rolls, chow mein, and chop suey which were the staples of restaurants outside of Chinatown. The herbal shops carried Asian healing remedies and health tonics not found anywhere else in the U.S. Other businesses provided services for Chinese immigrants with limited English language skills who were unable to negotiate within the mainstream community. And of course, there were the curio shops catering to the many tourists who came to look at this "exotic" community. While most had parents who worked in restaurants or laundries, there were the privileged whose parents owned the businesses in Chinatown. While mentioned in the bios throughout the book, we highlight some of these businesses together with names of their offspring.

Sandra K. Lee: *CEO of Harold Lee and Sons, Inc.*

Lived in: Great Neck, N.Y.
Now living: California and New York; bicoastal
Occupation: CEO of Harold Lee and Sons Inc, the oldest insurance company serving the Chinese community located on Pell Street.

Biography: Sandra is the daughter of Andrew Lee. The family came from the Toisan villages. Sandy is the first woman CEO of this family business serving the New York community since 1888. She joined the brokerage in 1981 following a career as a registered nurse, and has grown the business to a nationwide company.

Accomplishments: Sandra graduated from the University of Rochester with a degree in history and education and the Helene Fuld School of Nursing in New York City. She is active in civic and business organizations on local, state and national levels . She is a David Rockefeller Fellow and served the US Small Business Administration under Presidents Clinton and

35

Bush. She has been the recipient of many awards and honors for her leadership in healthcare, insurance and small business issues. She was named by Crain's New York Business as the top 100 most Influential Business Leaders in 2002 and a year later the Top 100 Minority Business Leaders.

Gloria Yee: *Family owned several businesses in Chinatown which were left to the sons per Chinese custom*

Born: 1941
Lived at: 37 Mott Street, Chinatown
Now living in New Jersey
Grandfather: Chuck Sun Ng
Biography: My maternal grandfather owned several buildings in Chinatown and was owner of several family businesses in Chinatown. My father was manager of Wing Wo Chong grocery store on Pell Street and of the China Lane Restaurant on Mott Street. The family also owned Wing Wo Lung grocery store on Mott and Bayard Street and Chatham Square Liquor Store. Wu's Restaurant on Bayard and Mulberry Street was later opened and operated by my father. When my grandfather died, he believed in the Chinese custom of leaving his fortune only to his sons.

Experience: 37 (Mott) was home to many. As many as 10 of the families living there were related. We were known as the *37 crowd*. Many of us spent our summers at Bradley Beach, the summer time "resort" for Chinese families from Chinatown. 37 was the social and community hub for many of us growing up in Chinatown. For several years, the 37 crowd hosted a reunion in Bradley Beach for everyone in our age group and their families. The kids got to go to the beach and we had a pot luck supper with roast pig (of course). It was enjoyed by all.

Clifford Lee: *Quong Yuen Shing—"Chinatown post office"*

This is an abbreviated story written by Clifford Lee about his granduncle, father, and the Quong Yuen Shing or *Chinatown Post Office*..

I was born in 1939. By the time I met Lee Lok, he was weakened by age and health. Shortly after that meeting, I attended his funeral. It was a huge Chinese funeral procession led by an Italian band playing somber music with a thundering drum. A man of Lee Lok's stature and position in the community meant having at least 3 funeral cars carrying flowers following

the hearst given by family members, family associations and business associates. The last flower car would have a huge portrait of the deceased. Immediate family members, close relatives and friends walked behind the last flower car. At the end of this very long procession was an open truck with Chinese musicians playing some melancholy melody. The funeral procession stopped at every place of importance to the deceased to allow his spirit to visit it one last time. This event from my childhood is etched into my memory of a family member who was an icon in New York City's Chinatown.

Biography of Lee Lok: Lee Lok, grandfather of John Mok, and granduncle of Clifford Lee, was revered by all of his relatives for his benevolence, wisdom and leadership. The Quong Yuen Shing store that he built in 1892 and continued under my father's management became an institution that served as a gateway to America for many from the Nam Village (Southern Village) in China.

We refer to him as "Gung" or grandfather out of respect. In 1879, my maternal grandfather, Lee B. Lok, at the age of 10, immigrated to San Francisco from China and then to New York with his uncle by way of a merchant ship. He then traveled to New York City, getting his first job as a dishwasher on the Bowery. By the age of 22, he joined an import/export firm, which in 1891 became a general store, Quong Yuen Shing & Co. This store served as a mail drop, herbal pharmacy, and exchange spot for money to China; it was known to many as the *Chinese post office*. In 1894, Lee Lok became head of the company, due to his ability to speak English. He paid $1,000 to upgrade his identity papers from coolie to merchant status, hence exempting himself from the Chinese Exclusion Act of 1882.

Lee Lok then contacted his older brother Hok Do in 1902 to send Toy Kin (my father) over to the US to help him with the business. My father said he was riding a water buffalo in the field when he was summoned by my grandfather and told he was heading west. He was 16 at the time. My father traveled alone with a ticket tied to his clothing to identify his destination. Over time, Lee Lok became Toy Kin's benefactor and mentor.

Upon arrival in the US in 1902, he stayed in the *fong* (i.e., room) in the back of the store that was rented by the Lee Family Association to serve as living quarters for Chinese immigrant bachelors. There were few Chinese women here at the time given the Chinese Exclusion Acts. Lee Lok groomed his nephew Toy Kin (my father) to manage Quong Yuen Shing with the same type of training he himself had received. Lee Lok renovated the store into a marvel of carved mahogany shelves, cabinets, and drawers to store the many varieties of Chinese herbs. Over the counter, the pride and joy of Chinatown was an arch, fantastically carved with flowering trees,

and peacocks, and lucky bats, its surfaces still tinted with red and gold, the colors of wealth….Far from being merely decorative, these arches were strategically placed to ward off evil spirits; the tangle of carvings would confuse them in their inexorably straight path toward mischief within. He had constructed a maze of storerooms, cubbyhole offices, and sleeping lofts on top in the back of the store; the offices had some massive Victorian safes used to store launderers' money until it could be shipped back to families in China. The space provided sleeping quarters for Lee clan members. Most of the Quong Yuen Shing employees were bachelors; they ate and slept in the store. There was a large kitchen in the basement including a commercial stove that was used to cook the meals and a large sink to wash the dishes. One of the employees was assigned to be the cook. There were 2 bathrooms, one of which included a bathtub and shower, in the basement. Towards the front of the store in the basement was a pot belly stove for heating. When I was a little boy, I used to watch them pour the coal down the chute from the street and the employees would shovel it into a pile near the stove. Eventually, the heating unit was converted to natural gas.

Lee Lok was a pillar in the Chinese community. In addition to founding the Chinese Merchants Association (*On Leong Association*), he also became an officer in the Lee Family clan association. As his community stature grew, the Quong Yuen Shing business also grew. Although outwardly it was just a general store specializing in elegant silks and satins, it was also well-stocked, like other stores in the area, with vegetables, medicinal herbs, spices, and supplies for other Chinese businesses. The only time that the store was closed was on Chinese New Year. The wooden floor would be washed and saw dust would be spread on New Year's Eve. One of the counters would be decorated and a tray of Chinese sweets and goodies would be placed on it for visitors or guests to enjoy. Then they would set up a little Chinese dice game in the back of the store. It was the only time that Lee Lok or Toy Kin would allow the employees to gamble within the store's confines. New Year's would be celebrated for a week and then it was back to business.

Lee Lok foresaw the need for more storage space for the operations to grow. He bought 7-8 Chatham Square to serve as a warehouse, enabling his to benefit from volume discounts. He shrewdly bypassed the NYC ordinance prohibiting people to sell property to Chinese citizens, using Toy Kin's citizenship to do so. Toy Kin was assigned the job of bill collection. He felt honored that Lee Lok entrusted him with expense paid trips to Boston. Philadelphia, Baltimore and Washington DC to collect on the bills from customers.

Warner Lai-Ong: *Owner of Luke Yum*

Born: 1940-1992
Father's Occupation: laundry owner and then farmer
Mother's Occupation: laundry owner and then a business owner of Luke Yum Restaurant Supplies and Wholesale Vegetables
Occupation: Co-owner of Luke Yum, family business
Biography: Born in Toisan, China and came to America in 1950 at the age of 10. During his childhood years, he lived in 96th Street and Park Avenue area where his parents and uncle

operated a Chinese Hand Laundry. He was drafted at the age of 18, and served in the U.S. Army from 1958-1960. When he returned home from the Army his parents moved to NYC Chinatown. After he married, he and his wife Anna were one of the early Chinese families to move to Queens.

Accomplishment: He started a restaurant supplies business on Bayard Street in NY Chinatown with his mother. The business, Luke Yum, supplied restaurants and grocery stores in the tri-state area with fresh vegetables, dried and canned goods and eventually expanded to the Bowery. It was primarily a wholesale business dealing in vegetables grown in New Jersey. Eventually, he contracted with a farm in Santo Domingo to grow the vegetables and have them shipped to NYC. He was the first to start this type of wholesale vegetable distribution business in NYC Chinatown.

Clan Associations and Community Leaders

While families were largely Toisanese Chinese with very similar backgrounds and origins, factions within the community did emerge among the different clan associations. The Chinese Consolidated Benevolent Association (located on Mott St where Wah Keuh Chinese School is) was and is an umbrella organization of 60 member organizations representing a cross-section of New York's Chinese community. This includes professional and trade organizations such as the Chinese Chamber of Commerce and the Chinese American Restaurant Association; civic organizations such as the American Legion, Lt. Kim Lau Post; religious, cultural and women's organizations; fellow-provincial organization such as the Hoy Sun Ning Yung Association; and family clan organizations such as the Lee, Eng, and Chan Family Associations being among the largest. *On Leong Tong*, otherwise known as the Chinese Merchants Association (located on Mott and Canal Street) was largely composed of Chinese businessmen in Chinatown; it played a prominent role among the community leaders in New York's Chinatown. These associations provided social services, personal and commercial conflict resolution and mediation services, promoted Chinese traditions and cultural heritage, and served as a bridge between Chinese American immigrants and mainstream groups. They sponsored educational and recreational activities, e.g., the boat rides, the Miss Chinatown contests, and the Wah Keuh Chinese School. Association. The officers became the community leaders of Chinatown who served as gatekeepers to mainstream America for a tightly knit and guarded community.

On a smaller scale, the family clan associations had similar purposes but were more localized to the needs of the family clan. In addition to the social networking they provided to the parents of our participants who came out weekly on Sundays to socialize at the clan associations, these clan associations also provided the economic supports in the form of employment, and small business loans or credit unions through a complex system known as *gung voy*. The clan associations originated as benevolent organizations of popular origin among overseas immigrant Cantonese Chinese communities for individuals with the same surname from the same villages.

The 1960s brought about a major change to the social and community structure in Chinatown. *Hip Sing Tong*, located on Pell St and known more for its association with Chinatown racketeering and drug trafficking fought a violent war for control of Chinatown's rackets and businesses with *On Leong Tong*. Both linked themselves with Chinese street gangs which led to unprecedented violence and robberies in Chinatown.

Many of the contributors to this book were only peripherally aware of these associations because their parents were the participants. A number of the contributors were the children of these community and business leaders who presided over the clan associations in Chinatown, e.g.,. **Danny (Skinny) Moy's** father was President of On Leong Tong. **John Mok's** grandfather, Lee Lok was founder of On Leong Tong. **Clifford Lee's** father presided over the Lee's Association, one of the larger clan associations in Chinatown as did **John K. Lee's** father who was Lee Bow. **Willie Eng's** father, Eng Bo Sing was a businessman in Chinatown presided over the Eng Association.

Phil Chin talks about his father who used to go to the clan associations on a daily basis. His father was active in On Leong Tong, Oak Tin Association; and Chin family association. He calls it the *Chinese Mafia*, referring to the clan involvement with the tong wars in 1960s, and various periods preceding the 1940s. **Lorraine Tsang** lived at 51 Mott St in Chinatown, and describes her mother going to play Mahjong in the associations downstairs, which Phil called the gambling dens of Chinatown. These are the same gambling parlors on which **Eugene Lee** did undercover work as vice squad as a police officer.

41

5 COMMUNITY NETWORKS: SHARED BONDS

Families, friends, and the community wove an intricate cobweb of relationships. Everyone knew one another. Many felt the eyes of relatives and friends on them who would report back to parents their ongoing activities in Chinatown. Relatives and neighbors watched over you. Chinatown was the community and provided a network of housing, employment, clan associations, social services, business services, and most of all ethnic and authentic Chinese Cantonese food that you could not get outside of Chinatown since most Chinese restaurants outside of Chinatown at that time catered to the tastes of its Western clientele. The community was more than those living in Chinatown as they were joined by the network of those coming into Chinatown weekly for social and community activities including: the Chinese Schools, churches, food shopping, and clan associations.

Since many had entered the country with false identity papers, fear and mistrust was rampant. A shroud of secrecy emerged that aligned with the Chinese taboo about discussing "bad things". At the same time, it violated Chinese cultural values of ethnic pride and integrity. Carrying on the family name remained important as apparent in the clan associations in the US replicating their villages in China; hence, children were often taught to use their true surnames with all matters Chinese, and their paper identity names in all matters American.

Ethnic pride and alienation manifested in the polarity between the *Jook Sing* who were American born Chinese vs. the *Jook Kock* who were born in China. Amongst them were the many elder bachelors who had come with dreams of returning to China, hence, the *sojourner*. Many of them had wives back in China, but were separated because of the anti-Chinese exclusion acts discussed earlier.

Many remember all the hangouts where they gathered for social activities of the Chinese-Americans. Though simple and even mundane in the memories, they reflect the shared bonds of friendships and community that was sustaining amidst the challenges of discrimination, poverty, and limited access to mainstream America.

Being Chinese

Chinese School was many things to this group. Learning Chinese was only one of the goals; some took it seriously while others saw it "as a joke". Most praised it for the long lasting friends they made. Mostly, it was about being Chinese-American. As **Harry Woo** exclaimed at the Kick Off event for this project, "We can do it; that's what they taught us in Chinese school; Don't give up. Many of the Asian American leaders today came from southern China, Guangzhou!" **Gladys Chin** reminded us of the emotion associated with people telling their stories, "one guy broke down when talking about the bullying by the Italians. Many are not here anymore to tell their story".

Lucy Leung: My parents said we should marry Chinese.

[At the Kick Off event], I am so glad to be here; these stories are important for the next generation. My brother, **Gilroy Chow**, continues to tell the story of the Chinese; he lives in the south now; and continues to record our contributions to the American culture. We had a good life now because of our parents. We need to give back for the goodness of what our parents sacrificed; there are fewer and fewer of us.

My parents said we should marry Chinese. In this generation, we don't tell our children that. I have three children; 2 children married Anglo Saxon, Caucasians; my other son met a Toisanese girl on Match.com. They're going to get married, and we were so happy to welcome her to the family. Her parents speak fluent Toisanese. She makes all the traditional foods—the kind that we know.

Anna Ong Shu: I traveled the subways at age 9 to attend Chinese School

Born: 1942
Lived in: Brooklyn, NY
Now living in: New Jersey
Biography: My maiden name Lee and also Lau; I came from Brooklyn. In the 1950s, I started Chinese School. I skipped first grade and graduated from the sixth grade in 5 years. My mother took me by subway for 6 months until I was 10 years old when I traveled by myself. I got to

know people socially at Wah Keuh—friends that I still have today. Chinese School started at 5PM and ended at 7PM, 5 days a week. We would get something to eat after American School ended, and take the subway (from Brooklyn to Manhattan). It was tough; my parents expected me to go, but I never complained. I was in the Drum, Bugle, and Fife Corp at Chinese School.; I was a Fifer and then a Twirler.

After I graduated, I continued to go to Chinatown to meet with friends. A lot of us got together regularly at City Hall bowling. We went to George Washington Baths in Coney Island every Tuesday or Wednesday. during the summer, and to Wollman Memorial Ice Skating Rink in Central Park in the winters. The boat rides to Bear Mountain hosted by the restaurant association was a big place to go at $5 for the day. We would always see a lot of people who we knew at these places. My life would have been very different if not for Chinese school since there were few Chinese people where I lived in Brooklyn.

The Jook Sing Generation

The *Jook Sing generation*—those American born Chinese of Chinese immigrant parents largely make up the contributors to this book—those growing up in NYC Chinatown during the 1940s-1960s. They are the first group to shed the shrouds of their immigrant backgrounds and limited socioeconomic resources. They were the first to escape, as many would exclaimed, from the bondage of their parents to laundries and restaurants. They were the first to assimilate in professions in mainstream America. Often they were the child interpreters for their non-English speaking parents of both the English language and the American culture. Their biggest challenge was that of maintaining their Chinese heritage while negotiating their assimilation and success in mainstream America.

The *Jook Sing* generation was polarized against the *Jook Kocks*. The label of *Jook Sing* (or the hollow and empty part of the bamboo) was a derogatory term to depict American born youth as lacking in Chinese culture and language and comparing them to the more urbane and "intelligent" *Jook Kocks* (or the knot of the bamboo). This polarity was a form of internalized prejudice stemming from the challenges assimilating to a hostile US society. The *Jook Kocks* often felt demeaned by the oppression of racial discrimination and limited opportunities and socioeconomic mobility; they remained proud of their Chinese heritage while trying to negotiate the vast differences in culture and language. The *Jook Sings* came to embrace this pejorative label as a *badge of honor*, proud that it reflected their sense of identity and ability to assimilate to American society.

All the contributors in this book have fond and vivid memories of the community and social activities in Chinatown that shaped their formative years and instilled in them a sense of their Chinese heritage and values.

Most had shared experiences and memories of the social activities and hang-outs covered by **Daniel Lee** in Chapter 3. The churches—Transfiguration and True Light, the Chinese Schools especially Wah Keuh Chinese School, the dances by the Jade Club and Four Seas in Chinatown, and at China Institute and McBurney's YMCA outside Chinatown, the boat rides to Bear Mountain, the bowling alley, the pool room, Washington Baths at Coney Island, Wolman Memorial Ice Skating in Central Park, and etc. Though many began to form social groups or "crowds" which hung out together, together they share common memories of the "good old days" when Chinatown was safe, and opportunities for meeting those like themselves, other Chinese friends, were robust.

While all have fond memories of their hardworking parents, and the values instilled by their parents through messages that they frequently heard, several remarked on how they lived in *basically fatherless homes or were latch key kids* because their fathers, and often their mothers, were working 6 ½ days a week. As Lenny Loo said, "we basically raised ourselves 75% of the time".

And yet, most have gone on to be upstanding U.S. citizens, and productive and successful professions—mostly in the fields of engineering, accounting, information technology, and K-12 teacher education. A number were exceptions in choosing fields where few Asians had ventured, and are chronicled in Chapter 10.

George Kwong: One of the *"kai doys"*

Nickname: Sleepy George
Year Born: 1940
Lived at: Chinatown
Father's Occupation: owned buildings in Chinatown
Biography: I was born in the Bronx and moved to Chinatown when I was 8 years old, and later to Kew Gardens in Queens. We bounced around my father's businesses, and laundry. My high school classmates were Simon and Garfunkel. When I turned 18, I moved into NYC, Chinatown. My father owned some cold water flats, 2 buildings in Chinatown on East Broadway and on Division Street; these were the railroad type apartments.

Experiences: I was nicknamed Sleepy George after one of the 7 dwarfs and a "proud" member of the *kai doys* in Chinatown. My life in Chinatown started about 1958; I lived there till about 1967. During that time, I was one of the "bad boys", the *kai doys*. We were associated with the pool room and the bars. The pool room on Doyers Street had most of the *Jook Kocks* (immigrants from the old country) and the one on Mott Street. had the *Jook Sings* (those from the new country). The actual meaning of *Jook Kock* is the node of a bamboo while the empty part is the *Jook Sing*.

We represented the bad kids of Chinatown in that era between the 1950s to 1970s. I worked in Lonnie's Coffee Shop for a couple of years serving coffee and hamburgers. Somehow I always made extras [portions] because these guys (my friends) would yell at me for giving them the lesser quality meat; I had to give them doubles or they would squeal on me. I made ice cream sodas, freezes, and whatever a short order cook would do. I think, I was working at Lonnie's when JFK got shot in 1962. After that I was in school trying to get another degree in engineering, taking engineering courses in all the schools in the area.

Lonnie's Coffee Shop

Lonnie's Coffee Shop in the center of Chinatown, was the hangout of the Chinese high school and younger college crowd on 21 Mott Street. It deserves attention in this book as the only place in Chinatown not serving Chinese food. It was more of a statement about the *Jook Sing* generation looking for a place and identity which they could claim as their own. Hanging out at Lonnie's Coffee Shop, the only "American" shop in Chinatown was symbolic for this *Jook Sing* generation of the bridge between their immigrant parents and mainstream society.

Valerie Tom: Do you know what a Lime Rickey is?

Year Born: 1944
Lived at: Mott St, Chinatown
Father's Occupation: Kwong Yee Wor grocery store
Biography: Valerie's family owned Kwong Yee Wor, a grocery store on Pell Street. Her aunt owned Lonnie's Coffee Shop. She still lives above the original store in Chinatown. Lonnie's was the favorite hang-out among the Chinese-American crowd, despite its limited menu, because it was the only store in Chinatown with western food. The crowds on Sundays, especially after church, was shoulder to shoulder. The Lime Rickey was a drink made with ½ lime and seltzer.

Elaine Chu

Classic picture of Elaine at age 16 with her husband of more than 50 years in front of Lonnie's Coffee Shop in the 1950s.

Bradley Beach

How did the Chinese from Chinatown end up at Bradley Beach, New Jersey? John Chin below tells the story. It became the haven for many Chinese from Chinatown as the summer vacation spot.

John Chin: All the Chinese lived on Newark Ave

Nickname: aka JC
Age: 1941
Lived at: Mulberry St, Chinatown
Mother's occupation: Laundry
Now living at: Bradley Beach, NJ
Occupation: Engineer
Fond Memories: Many years ago, the missionaries took the Chinese kids from Chinatown as part of the Fresh Air Fund to Ocean Grove, New Jersey to stay there for the weekend. Soon, some families went to the next town, Bradley Beach, because they were able to rent a bungalow there. It was the only town that would rent to non-whites. The husbands and fathers worked all week, and then joined their families there. It started in the 40s; over the years, families bought houses there. All the Chinese families lived on Newark Ave which was the main avenue. Ocean Avenue was the next block over where all the Italians from Mulberry

Street in Chinatown bought houses. My family bought a house there.

Biography: My mother immigrated here on steamship with my older sister to meet my dad; my twin sister and I were born here. My father had established a laundry in Brooklyn. We lived in back of laundry. My father died when I was 2 years old. My mother could not handle all the work, so she had to give it up and we moved to Chinatown on Mulberry Street when I was 8 years old. I was in Boy Scouts, Drum Corp, pool hall; I did everything one would do in a small town. I'm retired now; I was an engineer. Back in our generation, all the boys went to engineering school; the girls became school teachers. The generation after us, they became doctors and lawyers.

Miss Chinatown Contests

These pageants were an important part of community life, in that no Chinese Americans were ever considered for the Miss America Pageants because they did not fit the image of an American beauty. Known for their "exotic" beauty, Chinatown created its own pageants to celebrate the beauty of our own.

Debra Chiu (Gong): Today's children do not understand how it was growing up in a Chinese community.

Nickname: Debbie
Year Born: 1936
Lived at: 44 Commodore Circle, Chinatown
Father's Occupation: Chinese Hand laundry
Mother's Occupation: Chinese Hand laundry, Garment factory worker

Biography: It was not easy growing up in a Chinese family that already had two girls. I was the third girl, but born in America! My parents worked hard providing us with the essentials. I appreciated their sacrifice to raise all six of us. My five brothers followed, and I am proud that several of them served in the Armed Forces. Today, three of them do the Honor Guard that escort military

personnel to their final resting place. All volunteer their time!

Fond Memories: I was the second Miss Chinatown, USA, first from the Chinatown area. I went to Chinese school there and participated in most of the social events since I was 12 years old! Some fond memories include: going to Chinese school after my regular English school in Brooklyn and taking the subway train to Canal Street to get there. It was the first time actually meeting other Chinese kids who were not relatives. With them, I developed lifelong friends. I also have fond memories being a part of the Teen Hops at Transfiguration Church, True Light and later at the college dances uptown including: Columbia University, China Institute, City College and McBurney's YMCA. The restaurant boat rides to Bear Mountain were also great fun as was attending the Chinese Christian conferences in New York, Pennsylvania, Massachusetts and Toronto, Canada!

Today's children do not understand how it was growing up in a Chinese community. Knowing my heritage and living outside of the Chinese community made me kind of "*special*" to those that I met. I have always been immersed in the "white" community, but they always view me as special or different. I have NOT faced any racial discrimination.

Chinese School

Though many went, not all graduated.

Usually placed in grades several years their junior, this reflected the fact that those living outside Chinatown came in daily by public transportation, often unaccompanied

Chinese School, circa 1956

by adults. Some as young as 7 years old were chaperoned by their older siblings. Though learning Chinese was the wish of their parents, their wish was to socialize, making lifelong friends along the way.

The Chinese School Drum, Fife, and Bugle Corp was but one of the

activities which bonded the group. While most were less than serious about performing, the Drum Corp did go on to win many awards as one of the only Asian American Drum Corps around.

Willie Lau: It was a commitment I made to my parents.

Year Born: 1941
Lived at: Brooklyn in Bedford Stuyvesant
Occupation: Accountant
Father's Occupation: Laundry owner
Mother's Occupation: Laundry and then garment factory worker
Fondest memories: They're all great memories.

I am one of few who graduated from Wah Keuh Chinese School. I learned the most; it wasn't difficult. It was a commitment I made to my parents; they wanted me to go and learn Chinese. I did well. I skipped 1st grade; in 2nd grade, I came out first. But as I got into the Chinatown scene, my grades declined; later, I got lazier or did not focus. I had no trouble graduating; if I had been more serious, I would have done better. What my mother taught me at home and what I

learned in Chinese school expanded my knowledge of speaking Chinese. I was fortunate to have a desire to learn.

Biography: When I got older, I worked in Chinatown at Harold Lee & Sons for a few years, which fortified my Chinese further. I was point guard for the Basketball team at True Light Church with Eugene Lee. I played the bugle as a soprano in Drum Corp. My friends were in Chinatown.

I went to Pace University and became an accountant. At Boys High School, the students were largely Black and Puerto Rican. I was captain of the Cheerleaders and ran track. I did not want to hang with my friends in Brooklyn because of the gangs. When they went to a Rumble, I did not participate; nor did they did force me. In the beginning, there was some discrimination toward me. They would make believe they spoke Chinese, call me "chink", make their eyes narrow and slanted eyes to mimic mine. They often asked, Where you are from? When asked, I would look the person straight in the face, and ask if they were curious or something, then it would be OK.

Louise Leong Dilger: Living on both "sides of the Square" makes me a true Chinese-American

Year Born: 1942

Lived at: Henry Street, Lower East Side

Experiences: I'm from the "other side" of Chinatown: Henry Street to be exact. In my youth, I was cut off from Chinatown by Chatham Square (aka Confucius Plaza). It was just as dangerous then to cross over as it is today. Indeed, with the today's traffic and the multiple-intersecting streets it's probably more dangerous. The Third Avenue Elevated Line train station which stretched across the Bowery provided safe passage for us, especially after I started Chinese School.

As a kid, the only time I ventured to the other side was to go to the movie theatre on the Bowery with my brothers. We weren't permitted to speak English in the home, but for 20 cents our English language was honed from weekly viewing of cartoons and cowboy movies. Our heroes were Roy Rogers, Gene Autry, The Lone Ranger, Whip Wilson, etc.. My movie ventures terminated abruptly when I contacted lice at the theatre. After that, my mother referred to the theatre as the lice theatre and sadly I never stepped foot in there again.

My brothers and I played in the streets, climbed the fire escapes behind the East Broadway buildings (behind the parking lot on Henry St.) and in the park under the Manhattan bridge on Market and Henry Streets. Later, when the city tore down some buildings behind P.S.1 to build the current playground, we played in the dirt and sand piles. After the projects were built in the complex by Madison Street, my brothers and I entertained ourselves by taking elevator rides in the 20 story buildings. During the summers, the older kids turned on the fire hydrant and hooked up water sprays for kids in the neighborhood to play in [instead of going to the pool or beach].

Louise Leong   Rose Chin
Washington D.C.

When I started school, the public schools did not have kindergarten classes. My brother Donald and I attended Five Points Mission nursery school on the corner of Catherine and Madison Streets, where we learned to speak English. I attended P.S.1 from 1st to 6th grade and P.S.65 (Charles Sumner Jr. High) from grades 7th to 9th. My elementary school classmates were mostly Italian until the projects were built and we had an influx of black students. On the other side of the Manhattan Bridge was the Orthodox Jewish community. I didn't have much contact with them because the kids went to private Hebrew schools. By junior high, I was in classes with Italians, Blacks, Puerto Ricans and various Eastern European kids. My friends were not of Chinese decent.

We didn't have Chinese restaurants on our side. Henry Street was more than half Italian. I learned to eat ham and Swiss cheese sandwiches with mustard on Kaiser rolls from Mr. John and Mr. Joe's grocery store. I ate knishes from the corner stand on Delancey and Essex Streets, and mashed potato and pizza sauce sandwiches from a grocery store on Hester Street at ten cents a pop. (All of these sections now are heavily Chinese as Chinatown has expanded well beyond its three block radius.) I didn't experience Chinese restaurants until after I attended Chinese School in fifth grade.

My life changed dramatically once I was immersed with *Chinese* kids and the Chinese community. I found friends who shared the same cultural upbringing that my mother tried to instill in me. Perhaps I was growing up and was more appreciative of my ethnic background. I developed many long lasting Chinese friends from the Chinese School Fife, Drum and Bugle Corp and from attending Washington Irving High School. My multicultural background living on both "sides of the Square" makes me a true Chinese-American. I am married to an Anglo but value my Chinese culture and ethnic background.

Reunions

There were many retreats and reunions including those in YMCA Silver Bay, NY near Lake George organized by **Allan Poy Yee**. Many now had

families with children. The Las Vegas Reunions, however, are probably the most memorable. Founded in 2000, they brought together those from NYC Chinatown as many became seniors. **Gladys Chin** initially organized these reunions biennially; **Richard Chu** took them over in 2013 and continues the tradition. They are pictured below.

Back in the 50's, Gladys was already in the New Jersey/New York circles directing social events and relationships when she got most of the Newark boys together with the NY Chinatown girls at Bradley Beach, NJ one summer. Many trips across the Holland Tunnel followed this initial get together. In turn, it was social reciprocity for a number of New York guys who went across the Hudson to date the New Jersey girls. The happy end result was that a number of close relationships and even marriages followed these social endeavors of the NJ/NY "Trans-Hudson Connections" (quoted by **Daniel Lee**).

Richard Chu: "Chinatown was like being in the center of the world"

Nickname: Dick
Year Born: 1946
Lived at: 37 Mott St, Chinatown
Occupation: Pharmacist
Father's Occupation: Pharmacist
Mother's Occupation: Registered nurse
Biography: I grew up in 37 Mott Street, lived there till I married,

summered in Bradley Beach, attended PS 23 and PS 130, and graduated Columbia University College of Pharmaceutical Sciences. I acquired my father's pharmacy in the early 70's and worked there until the mid-80s. The rent became prohibitive and we closed up shop. Chinatown Pharmacy was an anchor in the community as the only western type pharmacy during the 40s-60s. I worked retail for another 30 years until I received a position with the NYC Dept. of Health. I retired in 2010 and never looked back.

Fondest memory: Growing up in NYC Chinatown was like being in the center of the world. It was one big mostly happy family. There were disagreements between friends but they all seem trivial now. My friends are the same ones that I grew up with, only they are now 60 plus years older. We are not unique either. I now organize the biennial Las Vegas Reunions. Looking around at our last one in 2013, you will see many groups with similar experiences. We are tolerant and respectful of one another.

Unique experience: My father, James Hing Chu, along with Kang Chu were the owners of Chinatown Pharmacy. It was the first Chinese owned western style pharmacy in New York City and maybe in America. The pharmacy was much more than just a neighborhood drug store; it was a meeting place, social hangout and message center all in one. There was a small bulletin board by the front door where news of Chinatown was posted. The owners of the pharmacy were also the photo historians of Chinatown. I have tons of old pictures, negatives and reels of movies to prove it.

Chinatown Pharmacy was synonymous with The Chinese Community Club (CCC). The Chinese Community Club, with help of the Chinatown Pharmacy, held Chinese New Year ballroom dances, Christmas parties for the children of Chinatown and Spring Field Day including a baby parade. CCC also sponsored athletic teams and a Chinese New Year lion dance troop. The Chinatown Pharmacy and CCC became even more closely related when CCC moved from Pell Street to a basement location under the pharmacy. It was pretty incredible that there was so much activity happening in such a small place. I have been blessed to have lived in the most famous apartment house in Chinatown, 37 Mott Street. We lived in a magical place and during an unforgettable era. There will never be a better time or place to have grown up. I still cherish the friends I made over 60 years ago. We were taught to be better than others in order to compete in life. Our generation and the ones before us illustrated that Chinese Americans are a hard working group. This reputation is even more evident today.

Oral History Project at 2014 Las Vegas Reunion

The Oral History Project, an extension of the NYC Chinatown Las Vegas Reunions, attempts to capture the ambience, the fortitude, the struggles, and challenges of this generation (see history in Chapter 2). Pictures from the 2013 Kick-Off event and 2014 Reunion are included here.

COMMUNITY

CONNECTING
Connecting with old friends

COLLECTING OUR STORIES

6 EDUCATION: THE PATH TO SUCCESS

Many were the first to graduate from college in the family. Most spoke to the pervasive importance of education to their parents and within the Chinese community. It not only aligned with Confucian values, but also enabled this generation of Chinese Americans to move out from the laundry and restaurant businesses of their parents.

Uptown-Downtown Chinese

The contrast between the uptown vs. downtown Chinese was made in a book by Kwong & Miscevic (2005) on *Chinese America*. Many of the *downtown* Chinese took issue with its seemingly negative characterization of the Cantonese Chinese as lacking in culture, education, and couth. What the book failed to acknowledge was the *privilege* of the *uptown* Chinese whose families came from educated backgrounds, immigrated here for education, and with resources, contrasting against the peasant farmer escaping starvation. Ironically, the groups separated themselves geographically with Cantonese Chinese largely concentrated in downtown New York City while the northern (Mandarin and Shanghainese) Chinese largely concentrated in uptown Manhattan, near China Institute on the East 60s, again reflecting this difference in socioeconomic status.

Education for both groups was paramount, in alignment with Chinese Confucian values and culture, but for different reasons. The Cantonese Chinese saw it as an opportunity to escape the drudgery of the laundries and restaurants. The family business was generally not appealing as the place to join.

Daniel Lee: What's wrong with being Downtown Chinese?

Nickname: Danny
Lived at: 28-30 Division Street, Chinatown
Occupation: Electronic Engineer, ME, MBA, PE
Quote: A note of love and appreciation to my Mom and Dad for their strength and resiliency in teaching us, through everyday life examples of our Chinese family values and the importance of education. Our many church groups in Chinatown who provided the vital teachings and lessons to lead a good Christian life.

Accomplishment: Daniel Lee, in a conversation with Dr. Peter Kwong, and Dr Dusanka Miscevic, Columbia University about his book was posted on NYC Chinatown Oral History website (www.ceoservices.wix.com/nycchinatownoralhist). While finding their book *Chinese America: The untold story of America's oldest new community:* which he found to be very informative and fascinating history, he also found it to be disturbing and alarming because of the many references to the *Uptown Chinese and the Downtown Chinese*. He felt this terminology, used repeatedly throughout the book, made derogatory innuendos about the Downtown Chinese, defined as the southern Chinese who spoke Cantonese, and the Uptown Chinese defined as the northern Chinese who spoke Mandarin.

"While I respectfully disagree with your concept of Uptown and Downtown Chinese which was mentioned more than 58 times in the book, I offer merit based *"vivid living memories"* and *"actual life experiences"* from the Chinatown era of the 40's to the 60's when our generation, children of southern Chinese immigrants, started to break out of the perceived Chinatown cultural barrier to counter your many negative assertions. Education was the catalyst and express lane into the professional world of mainstream America". He points to the Introduction (page xv) where Drs. Kwong and Miscevic describe:

"The superbly educated, urbanized, English-speaking representatives of the upper stratum of Chinese society who avail themselves of this opportunity formed an Uptown Chinese community, at the opposite end of the social hierarchy from the working-class immigrants from rural southern China. The liberal 1965 immigration reform opened the door to a two-pronged migration of Chinese from both ends of the spectrum: the professional at the top, and the relatives of earlier immigrants at the bottom. The latter provided cheap labor for the services and declining industries, in particular garment manufacturing. Chinese America became a distinctly bipolar entity. The two groups, the Uptown and the Downtown Chinese have little in common. Their different experiences make classification under a single model of integration in America meaningless".

Daniel Lee recounts his experiences growing up in NYC's Chinatown in his rebuttal to Drs. Kwong and Miscevic. "I am a product of the NYC Chinatown community of the 40's to 60's where many of us did not have a lot in material assets but did have the tenacious energy and determination, in a tough competitive environment to achieve success through education. It is this tenacity and ambition to excel that we overcame many obstacles and went on to enter various professional fields of engineering, science, medicine, law, education, and finance etc. Even as far back as middle school in Chinatown and Little Italy, we came to realize that we had a smart group of Chinese kids, both academically and talented in the arts. Of the twenty or so Chinese kids in my class, we were all accepted by entrance exams to attend Stuyvesant High School, Bronx High School of Science, or Brooklyn Technical High School. A few also got accepted at the High School of Music and Art and Hunter College High School. Back in those days of the 50's, I did not recall seeing or meeting any Uptown Chinese kids at Stuyvesant High School. It was probably because the Uptown Chinese kids were either in private schools or not old enough for high school since their parents were still graduate students (stranded scholars) or just getting started in their professional careers before having a family.

College for the Chinatown kids was mostly at City College, Queens College, Hunter College, Baruch College, and Brooklyn College. For the families that could afford it, there were educational opportunities in the Ivy Leagues and polytechnic institutes: Columbia University, Stanford University, University of California, New York University, Massachusetts Institute of Technology, Rensselaer Polytechnic Institute, Brooklyn Polytechnic Institute, etc. While in college as an engineering student, I was also intentionally involved in all types of extracurricular activities with the goal of learning, through real life experiences, the many complex personalities of people and their social interrelationships.

When I was at Grumman Aerospace Corp. on Long Island, in the early 60's, working as an Electronic Engineer on the Apollo Program to land a man on the moon, it was a proud experience being Chinese American. At this early stage of my career, it was extraordinary to see so many Chinese American engineers, throughout the Grumman Aerospace Center working on this important program of national interest in competition with the USSR's space efforts. The Thermodynamics group had 40 engineers of which 4 were Chinese Americans which was 10% of the group; this was at a time when the Chinese population in the U.S. was probably 1%.

All of the Chinese American engineers at the time at Grumman were the children of Downtown Chinese immigrants living throughout the NY Metropolitan area, who originally came to America as laborers or merchants. With all due respect to the Uptown Chinese at the time, they were probably still in graduate school; engaged in other professions, or were unable to acquire the necessary levels of security clearances required for this vital national security aerospace program of the decade." Hence, he objects to the quote by Kwong & Miscevic (p. 232):

> *"The influx of political refugees, the stranded scholars, and the Taiwan-and Hong Kong-trained professionals produced a new community of Chinese Americans, as escapees from Communist rule or products of the anti-communist bastion of Taiwan; these Chinese had impeccable anti-communist credentials- They were the "good Chinese" These "Uptown Chinese" had very little in common with the early immigrants from the semirural regions of southern China, who were mainly working-class restaurant, laundry, and sweatshop employees. They did not even converse in the same dialect--most Uptown Chinese were from the North and spoke Mandarin or Shanghainese, while the Downtown Chinese spoke Cantonese. And they certainly did not reside in the same neighborhood. Most Downtown Chinese were isolated in ethnic ghettos, while the uptown Chinese moved into affluent integrated city neighborhoods or to the suburbs"*

Daniel's initial reaction was: What is wrong with being a working class restaurant, laundry, and sweatshop employees when it is an honest living and providing support for a family and putting food on the table? Presumably, the ethnic ghetto was NYC's Chinatown where southern Cantonese Chinese families lived and relatives and friends would visit on Sundays' to socialize and spend quality time together. It should be noted that the northern Mandarin Chinese also came down to Chinatown on Sundays' to shop for Chinese groceries, pastries, and supplies at specific markets that cater to them. Sunday was always a festive day in Chinatown where many families (Uptown Chinese and Downtown Chinese alike) enjoyed Tea and Dim Sum for lunch and supper at the local restaurants. The common denominator is that everyone has to eat and Chinese food is always freshly prepared, delicious, and appreciated for its best value whether you are a northern or southern Chinese.

Not an uncommon story is the working class restaurant worker who teams up with several other workers to open up a restaurant is well known. Their entrepreneurialism through hard work and tasty value meals leads to success. Soon the owner(s) buy the building in which the restaurant is located to expand the growing business. As time passes, the owner(s) start to buy up the other buildings on the block and collect rent from neighboring store owners. To live the American dream, a house is then purchased for the growing family. Along the way, a few other houses are purchased providing more positive cash flow.

The Exam High Schools

Most of the Chinese from Chinatown attended Haaren High School, Washington Irving High School, or Transfiguration High School, the feeder public schools to Chinatown. And then there was the exam public high schools. As **Daniel Lee** and John Mok both recount, they went with a group of their peers, but remained very much the minority at Stuyvesant and Brooklyn Tech High Schools. **John Mok** says, I went to Stuyvesant High School; there were seven of us—Chu, Chang, Chin, Moy, Mok, Lee; the rest were Jewish compared to today where 70% of Stuyvesant students are Chinese. **Park Gong, Daniel K. Moy, Ed Chin, Henry Hum, and Joe Chu** all went to Brooklyn Tech High School and remain friends to this day.

The City Colleges

Private colleges were for a select few; most of those who did went to New York University or Columbia University. The vast majority went to one of the city colleges which today are part of the City University of New York; the Chinese went primarily to City College or Hunter College although some went to Brooklyn College or Queens College. I was one of 3 Asian Americans at Brooklyn College when I attended in 1962. These colleges were tuition free at the time, and responsible for many being able to get a college education. This led to the forming of the Chinese Intercollegiate Club which hosted dances across the colleges, and continued the community networks among the college groups.

Mary Sham: descendant of laborer who helped to build the transcontinental railroad

Occupation: School Teacher
Born and raised on Pell St; Chinatown
Biography: I went to P.S. 23. When I was in the second grade; my father went to Hong Kong to study Chinese; we ended up staying there for 10 years. When I was in JHS, we got notification to return to the US. I then went to Washington Irving High School, and ; then to Hunter College where I got my BA and became a teacher. I went back to P.S. 23 to teach.
Unique Experience: As many as 12,000 Chinese American labourers helped build the transcontinental railroad, predominantly on the West Coast. Working for a fraction of the pay of their non-Asian White counterparts, these "coolie" laborers were assigned some of the most dangerous tasks. Unknown numbers of Chinese American men lost their lives in the course of laying the railroad, in part because of ongoing anti-Asian racism among the work crews. White laborers viewed their Chinese American colleagues with disdain, calling them "midgets", "effeminate" and "monkeys". Yet, when

the railroad was completed on May 10th, 1869, an event commemorated in a historical photograph that showed actual railroad workers crowded around the final spike as it is hammered into the ground, Chinese American laborers were conspicuously left out of the photograph.

Corky Lee re-created this photo on May 10, 2014 at the Golden Spike National Historic Site in Tremonton, Utah, this time with the faces of Asian America front and center! Mary Sham joined him in that momentous event as her grandfather had been one of the workers on the transcontinental

railroad. "I was the most senior person there! she says

Accomplishment: I was the Vice President of Education at the Organization of Chinese Americans – Long Island. I got a scholarship program going through the Gates Program for Chinese students who wanted to go to college, but could not afford it. I am very proud of that. I am also proud of my accomplishment to speak both Chinese and English.

7 FROM LAUNDRIES AND RESTAURANTS TO TEACHERS AND ENGINEERS

The majority of the fathers of this generation were either restaurant workers or laundry owners. Upon arrival in the U.S., most found ways to survive through the only occupations allowed to them—the Chinese hand laundries and Chinese restaurants.

Cantonese Chinese food, initially known as exotic, included westernized dishes of Chow Mein, Fried Rice, Chop Suey, Egg Rolls, Fortune Cookies—none of which are generally eaten by the Chinese. And though Cantonese cuisine is considered the gourmet cuisine in China, the flurry of these Chinese restaurants provided inexpensive tasty Chinese food.

Those living outside Chinatown were often families with Chinese hand laundries where families lived in the back of the laundry—sharing sleeping quarters with the family business. Children generally participated in helping the parents with such tasks as stamping tickets, wrapping the cleaned laundry in brown paper packages, ironing handkerchiefs and shirt sleeves. This started as young as 6 years old. The mothers often worked side by side with their husbands in the laundries.

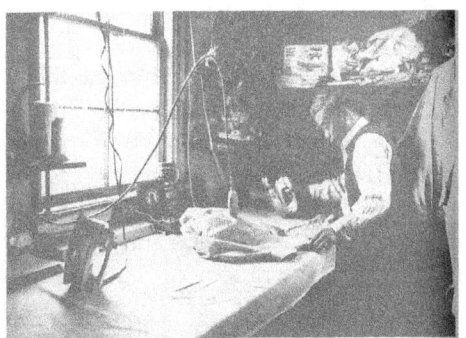

Later, as laundries began to decline (with the availability of washing machines and wash and dry dress shirts), they went on to work in the garment factories, also known as the sweat shops in Chinatown. To make ends meet, many of the women also did piecework costume jewelry beading.

While children often go into the family business, the message of most Chinese immigrant parents was their wish that their children would "not have to toil in the laundry, and have a life of such drudgery. Most children got this message loud and clear. As **John Chin** said, "the guys became engineers, the girls became teachers".

Gene Woo: It's a long journey. We needed to persevere and continue to move forward.

Year Born: 1948
Lived at: Baxter Street, Chinatown
Occupation: Electrical Engineer
Father's Occupation: Waiter in restaurant
Mother's Occupation: Homemaker
Biography: My grandfather had a laundry on 105 Street. When I went to City College; I would go there after class to visit him. As a little kid, I never saw his laundry because it was up in Harlem. I didn't realize how hard it was until I visited.
I enjoyed growing up in Chinatown. I played baseball, stickball. All the families would come down at night during the summer to stay cool; in the park. My sister Betty Leong, now a retired school teacher, was not allowed to Mott Street until high school because she was a girl.. At home, my father worked morning till night; we never saw him. I didn't know Chinatown had the cheapest places to live. We got by. One of my mom's enjoyment was going to the Chinese movies each weekend. It was only 10 cents for children then, and 25 cents for adults then.
Unique experience: I was the first Asian American to be mayor within the NYC area as the former Mayor of Plandome Heights, NY. The reason I got involved was to show an Asian face. My college graduating class at City College was the first wave of Chinese Americans going to college. During that time, President John F Kennedy said we would land a man on the

moon by 1970; every boy wanted to be an engineer. Out of my whole high school class, only two made it. I remember my engineering professor during my freshman year told us to look around, and note that your neighbor will probably not be there next year; out of the 300 College freshmen, only 15 graduated as engineers. I got involved in Chinese Culture Club in college and organized the first Chinatown street cleaning.

Impact of growing up in Chinatown: There were challenges and success stories. There was always the unspoken idea that I was supposed to get a good education; my job was to study. It was the negative challenges that made me. As an American-born Chinese, when I went into Chinese restaurants and not speak good Chinese, they always made fun of me. That made me resilient. At the same time, pressures outside Chinatown from the gangs of territorial groups all there protecting their block elicited fear when we passed through. My goal was to get a good education and get out of Chinatown to the suburbs; that was everyone's goal! My parents were not strict; they didn't have to be since I knew my job. My father was not a gambler and didn't want us going to the gambling dens which he called "alligator pits".

Fondest Memories: playing in the backyard on Baxter Street; it was a parking lot then; now it's a hotel; going to Chinese banquets; hanging around in Chinatown Fair, the bowling alley and pool room.

Discrimination: Elementary school was in Chinatown with mostly Chinese at P.S. 23; going on past that where you had to go outside Chinatown which was not our territory, we would get jumped. To protect ourselves, we would walk in groups so it would be harder for them to attack. You always had to walk around as if you're ready to fight, i.e., macho.

Gingee Moy: We knew we didn't want to stay in the laundry

Lived at:
Occupation: K-12 School Principal
Father's Occupation: Laundry
Mother's Occupation: Laundry
Biography: Gingee is one of the few to become a school principal. Others included: **Elsie Chan, Helen Chin, Accomplishment:** Growing up in the back of a Chinese hand laundry, and helping my parents in the laundry, we knew we didn't want to stay in the laundry.

Helen   Chin
and
Elsie Chan

Jean Marie Chin: My parents always told us to behave as a good citizen because "you're Chinese".

Born 1941
Lived: Flushing, NY
Occupation: K-12 Principal
Parents' Occupation: Laundry

Biography:

I grew up in Manhattan up until I was 8 years old. My parents had a laundry. When my father passed away when I was very young, we moved to Flushing. Back then, there were only maybe three other Chinese families My other Flushing Chinese neighbor, Lucy and I became good friends and went to the dances together. Though I did not live in Chinatown, it means a lot to me. I only started going down to Chinatown because I was looking for a social life in my late teens. So I heard of the clubs and went down to Transfiguration and a few of their affairs. Through a retreat, I met my husband and we've been married for 52 years. We got married young. We had kids right away.

Accomplishment:

I went back to school for my BA in my late 40s after my children finished college; I got an MA degree, and became a school principal when I was 50. There was housing discrimination. When my mother tried to buy a house in Queens, the realtor wouldn't sell us the middle house; I was told "because then I can't the house on either side".

I was a principal at a late age; I decided to go back to school at 48; I was one of the older college students—one of the lucky ones to go to college with scholarship. It's about resiliency—when you grow up with the insecurity as Chinese-American. As I matured, I gained more confidence in myself. We need to tell our story before everyone's gone. When I first started in education, I was a counselor with Chinatown Planning Council. I asked a girl whose teacher was a Chinese man. I told her she was the lucky one with a man teacher who was Chinese. She said, he's not Chinese; he doesn't speak Chinese. These young Chinese think you're not Chinese if you do not maintain the culture; it's important to know where you came from.

8 DISCRIMINATION: INTERNAL AND EXTERNAL

These remembrances and stories are filled with themes of discrimination. While Chinese Americans are often viewed as the "model minority", it is often assumed that they experience little discrimination. Intense anti-Chinese sentiment diminished over time, especially after WWII because the Japanese became the new enemies of the U.S. As described in Chapter 4, Chinatown was the safe haven from external discrimination. Those living outside Chinatown were often the "lone" Asians in their neighborhoods. This continued to be true as this generation ventured on to college and careers, housing and socializing. As discussed in Chapter 5, discrimination also occurred from within as this *Jook Sing* generation distinguished by its lack of the Chinese culture.

While bullying from the Italians occurred, it was largely targeted toward the boys. As **Helen Chin** notes, "the girls did not have the same problems as boys". This is confirmed by **Susan Eng** who says, "Even if there was prejudice, we were often not aware of it; I did not experience the name calling".

Combat Zone–Little Italy

Though adjacent to one another, Chinatown and Little Italy were two different worlds. Chinatown with Mott Street as its main street ran parallel to Mulberry Street, the next block over and the main street of Little Italy. Crossing Canal Street was the real division between the two cultures. Experiences were mixed with a large group, mostly males, consistently having been bullied as children by the Italians. They were teased, beaten up, and bullied, and for some, leaving life-long scars. For others, groups of Chinese boys grouped together for protection while others ran for their life after school to escape the physical terror that might befall them.

The bullying and discrimination stemmed from intolerance of difference. Groups who themselves felt marginalized also made the Chinese scapegoats; what better way to bolster one's self esteem than to pick on another group with less power. Some made friends with the Italians as contact with one another led to shared experiences of trying to make a go of it as immigrants. Ironically, the two groups ended up owning summer homes in the same town of Bradley Beach, New Jersey, again separated by one block on Newark Ave and Ocean Ave.

Daniel Lee: The great divide of Canal Street

Experiences: Looking back through my narrow prism of time (late 40's-mid 60's) and those of my close friends and classmates at the New York Chinatown of the 50's and 60's, one can see a close and small community where everyone basically knew one another, did a lot of things together, and looked after one another at times. The teachings and influences of our *Chinese family values*, coupled with the *moral compass* instilled in us by the teachings of the respective church groups and their related activities cannot be over emphasized. Many friendships developed back then are still intact today, having survived the distance drums of time serving as testimony to the *strength and bond* of the relationships formed.

Next in the educational line was the *"physical combat zone"* of **PS 130** for 7th and 8th grades on the corner of Hester and Baxter Streets in Little Italy. It certainly was a diversified and engaging two year experience in human interaction and explicit exposure to racial discrimination. Here at PS 130, we were the minority, whereas; we had been the majority at PS 23. In addition to receiving a normal education, we were going through a big social transition with regard to abusive language usage, forward female behaviors and aggressive male attitudes, and at times, even practicing the art of self-defense. It was certainly a different slice of the experiences and *"life lessons learned"* in true living color in comparison to the PS 23 environment in Chinatown.

Physical Combat Zone: In a conversation with **James Yee Gan Moy**), they recall "Welcome to Little Italy" on the first day at JHS PS130 by way of a fight. Vinnie was lying in the closet when our home room teacher finally showed up. It was like the movie *Blackboard Jungle*. We concentrated on taking care of the leader—a kid named Anthony Marino *Tiger*. Once he was neutralized, everything fell into place for a shaky and respectful relationship between us Chinese and the Italians, with less confrontations.

In retrospect, our JHS PS 130 experience were like the "school of hard knocks"; it made a lot of us "street smart" to survive the challenges that were ahead for us in life—both physically and mentally. There were stories about this young boy *Gawk Giet* (**Robert Gong**) running for his life every day after school at JHS PS 130 to reach the *great divide of Canal St*—to cross over from Little Italy to the safety of Chinatown. Later on in life, he had a jewelry business on Mott Street next to Ernie Mar's Mandarin Dress and Gift Shoppe. Robert did very well in business and was always dressed impeccably; he became a smooth talker to round out his persona. I venture to think that most of the Italian kids that used to chase him wound up in jail or got mixed up with the Mafia, *La Cosa Nostra.*

Daniel Lee notes the proper respect **James Yee Gan Moy** received "when you took care of the "music sheets snatcher" in your wrestling bout with all the other Italian kids watching. They were shocked that this violin playing Chinese Kid could hit back and hold his own". **James Moy** notes: I played the violin in the school orchestra. Mrs. White, the Director, gave some music sheets to this Italian boy to pass on down to me. He looked at me, and said, "I'll give them to you outside." "You can fight for it" was implicit in his comment. "OK," I said. As an 8th grader, I had been taking boxing lessons from Calvin Gum, and I had been weight lifting in the Chinatown Barbell Club for a whole year. Big and strong like an Ox at that age, I had no fear. I went outside during the lunch hour, and there was about 20 other Italian boys ready to jump me. One of my Italian friends at that time was Big Joe, a 14 year old Italian immigrant who was about my size. He took charge, held the other kids back, and said: "We're going to have a fair fight!" This was all he needed to say. The pack stayed out, and I had an easy time wrestling with the boy. Joe and I came back late to class with huge smiles on our faces. All the kids knew what had happened, and they cheered when we walked in. I don't think the teacher knew what was going on. It's amazing how we survived those years.

Intellectual Combat Zone: After PS 130, many of us were fortunate enough to be accepted by competitive exams to attend NYC's specialized academic high schools and a number of us went to **Stuyvesant High School** where we now entered an *"intellectual combat zone"* for the next four years. In the 1950's, Stuyvesant was an all boy school like **Brooklyn Technical High School** where the best and brightest competitive male students came from all over the city. **Bronx High School of Science** was the only co-ed school of the specialized academic high schools in the 50's. Stuyvesant even had a split session, which afforded us an opportunity to have a part time job and to even participate in school athletic programs after school.

College was where our friends and classmates went in different directions to study science, engineering, medicine, law, business, finance, ministry, education, social sciences, etc. at various colleges and universities. After college it seemed like the professional, economic, and social worlds all opened up at once (60's). Being gainfully employed as a electronic engineer had many advantages since we now finally had some money and were fortunate enough to work on America's1960's aerospace challenge of putting a *"man on the moon"* (**Apollo Lunar Program**) while still attending graduate school at night for my Masters, MBA, and Professional Engineer License, sponsored by the Grumman Aerospace Corp. on Long Island.

One of the initial family benefits of an engineer's salary was that I was able to move my Mom and Dad to the new Bridgeview Apartments, with all its modern amenities, at 50 Bayard Street--A *proud & happy moment for them* and a small token of love and appreciation on my part for all they had done for me over the years. Our *parents provided the guiding force and ever present inspirational model* for our family and they always encouraged my brothers and sisters to be the best... that we can be in everything we pursued in life.

It has been a long journey for many of us, *1st generation American Born Chinese (ABC)* who came from humble backgrounds and learned the *street smarts of* real life experiences in the crowded tenements and streets of Chinatown. For my classmates and friends who have passed through the NYC public schools, private schools, and on to college to pursue their professional fields of endeavor, it was quite an achievement when one considers all the obstacles that we had to overcome to enter the professional ranks of engineering, medicine, dentistry, law, business, finance, education, ministry, etc. These successful accomplishments were made possible by sacrifices from our parents and families through years of hard work and with our own burning desire to succeed in our chosen profession.

There were no entitlements or handouts along the way. A large number of us have moved to the other NYC Boroughs, Long Island, Westchester County, Connecticut, New Jersey and many other states throughout the country. One can only speculate what the Chinese American and Asian American population numbers, social standing, professional profile, and political influence and impact would be today in the United States if the racially biased exclusion acts had never been passed by Congress.

Donald Chin: Why did I have to be born Chinese?

Nickname: the Duck, Donald Duck
Born: 1944
Biography: I was born in Jersey City in NJ. We moved to Chinatown when I was less than one year old in 1944. My father was always either a restaurant worker or owned laundries at different addresses. I grew up in Chinatown and I know the early years of going to school, I wished my name was Donald, Gerald, or Sullivan. *Why did I have to be born Chinese?* There was a major persecution complex when you grew up in that area. But all the while, your parents reminded you of our culture, who we are. Subsequently, once we got into our adulthood, I know it is politically incorrect to say, but Chinese are really a very superior race in intelligence. I don't mean this to be racist, but I really felt after weighing out

the different factors, we really are a pretty superior intelligent race. And again I'm not trying to be racist. ("We're unique" as qualified by Skinny.)

Challenges: I, along with a couple of other people, **Hon Lee** is one of them, were one of the forerunners in the school. This is back in the 60s of the rapid advancement classes. We skipped the 8ᵗʰ grade. We went from 7ᵗʰ to 9ᵗʰ. Junior high school then high school. So we went to school away from Chinatown. And again, I would say, *How come I was born Chinese? Why couldn't I be born Irish? Why couldn't I be born White?* There really was a bias, as far as being a minority. As a minority, I can sympathize with other minorities, the plight that they go through. It is inbred in us, Chinese; we will prevail….. that we will survive. Let me pass it on to the mayor (referring to Skinny Danny).

Larry Lau: I was angry

Occupation: Commercial Artist
Lived in: Chinatown

Biography: My name is Larry Lau and I grew up in Chinatown and I was nothing but trouble growing up. Always getting in fights; the cops used to bring us home all the time. One time when I was sleeping, I got a knock on the door; it was [Daniel Moy-Skinny] and six other guys. They said "We're gonna join the Army." And I said "Okay let's go kill some Germans." I was very prejudiced at that time; the White people were too. "What's theirs is theirs, and what's yours is theirs!" If you went out with a girl who was pretty then, *their girls*, the men would get mad as hell at you. When I tried to go to swimming pools or stuff like that, they wouldn't let you in. I used to get into two fights a week. When you fight a white guy, make sure you beat them up twice as hard because they are so prejudiced.

When I got into the Army, it was the same thing. They always picked on the Asians; but, I was a little bit different from the other Chinese guys. I fought back. I put three of my sergeants into the hospital. I was always getting into trouble. [The Whites] blame us for WWII, they blamed us for the Korean War and they blamed us for the Vietnam War. So every time I used to get in a fight with White guy, I made sure that I put him in a hospital. [The situation has improved.] When I was young, they used to spit on us and kick us when you walked down the street. As I grew up, we'd get the hate. So I began to believe that every time somebody tries to kick you, you should break his leg.

Calvin Moy: They bullied my brother

Occupation: Truant Officer
Lived in: Chinatown
Memories: I walked the streets of Chinatown; it was friendly, everything was open. When walking outside Chinatown, that's when things happened.

Calvin recalls his brother always being bullied and beaten up. To this day, he has suffered long-term consequences from the beatings, having to go through surgeries because of injuries to his spine.

Joseph Chan: My biggest fear was being shot by friendly fire.

Nickname: Sweeney
Lived in: Chinatown
Biography: Came from a family of seven children, and grew up in Chinatown. He banded together with other Chinese Americans for safety and protection because they were bullied by the Italian kids. He enlisted in the Marines at age 17 to escape the confines of Chinatown. When the Korean War broke out, he fought on the frontlines for the U.S. His biggest fear was being shot in the back by one of his fellow marines—*from friendly fire.*

Where are you from?

As **Pearl Chow** and **Willie Lau** said, we were always being asked "Where are you from?" Always perceived as a foreigner, this form of discrimination persists today. Most of the contributors to this book recall being picked on, called derogatory names, and mimicking Chinese faces, often on a daily basis, by their classmates, neighbors, and people they meet.

For those living within the safety of Chinatown, they did not experience this until they left Chinatown. The perpetual question of "Where are you from?" was so common, "we often unwittingly answered *China* though we were born in the U.S." So common were this question that many identified ourselves only as Chinese, never viewing ourselves as Americans. It mirrored how we felt and were welcomed into American society. It was not until the Civil Rights Movement of the 1960s that our heightened sense of ethnic pride and identity led us to challenge these racist assumptions.

Paper Names

While the U.S. wanted cheap Chinese labor, Chinese were specifically barred them from entry to the U.S. via the many Chinese Exclusion Acts between 1882 and 1943. This was later replaced by a quota system again discriminating against Chinese. Many Chinese devised clever ways to gain entry through the purchase of papers alleging family ties which afforded entry to the U.S.

Most of the parents of this generation immigrated to the U.S. under an assumed name. U.S. immigration authorities were always aware of this practice, and set up intensive interrogation practices to detect the truth. Chinese went often detained at Angel Island or Ellis Island and scrutinized daily detention until they could be cleared. Interrogation questions included such minutia as the specific design and location of rooms in their homes and villages in China as well as a rundown of family membership in attempts to detect false information.

Once in the U.S., most retained both their paper names and real names since family lineage is so highly valued. Most associated with the clan of their real names. Despite this, most were hard working in making a living for their children; most did not expect to see the benefits of their hard labor for themselves as evident in their stories and messages of struggle and drudgery.

For years, the fear of deportation persisted if the government were to find out. This led to a shroud of secrecy and mistrust in the community that was only enhanced by an unwelcoming American society. It also provided the opportunity for exploitation by the authorities. Police in Chinatown would selectively exercise the Sunday blue laws by issuing summons to those businesses who had not paid a bribe. Chinese were stopped on the streets and asked for their identity papers. Police would raid Chinese businesses in search of "illegal" immigrants.

Yet, their children, contributors to this book, went on to successful professional careers, and upstanding U.S. citizens. Many served in the military and have made contributions to society.

Anne Lee: They made fun of my Chinese because I was Hakka.

Lived at: Mulberry St, Chinatown

Now living in: Chinatown
Occupation: School Teacher
Biography: Anne identifies as being Hakka
My father came first to the US before WWII
in the 1920s by ship. My mother came
through Ellis Island. We had paper names;
five of us were born after WWII. Our real
name is Yee not Lee. Our English last name
was Lee; our Chinese last name was Yee.
When we went to Chinese School, we knew

our last name was different; yet, we couldn't ask my mo because she spoke
no English; besides she was secretive about it. My family spoke Hakka, and
the kids in school would always make fun of my Chinese. I knew I was
right though when I spoke. (The Hakka was a wandering group from
northern China who fled to southern China during the Song Dynasty. The
term *hakka* was used to indicate "guests" who had left their homelands to
settle down in other parts of the country. Anne's treatment reflects some
of the ongoing internal discrimination faced among Chinese Americans.)

I'm a retired public school teacher, the first one in the family to go to
Hunter College and graduate. My parents were so proud because they
wanted us to get out of the laundry and restaurant business. My #2 brother
went to Stuyvesant High School.

9 RESILIENCY

Crash Landing

There were many ways to get to the U.S. In the early days, some came by steamship. Later they arrived by plane. Many came through Hong Kong from Toisan China. The entry points varied from Vancouver, Seattle, Mexico, Angel Island, California, and Ellis Island, New York as ports of entry. Many were illegal with purchased identification papers; others were not. All came seeking the opportunities of the Golden Mountain.

But it was the crashing landing that was the real test as these Cantonese Chinese faced language and cultural barriers, and lacking in socioeconomic resources. The banded together and sought refuge in Chinatown, which gave more than a place to live or a place to go. It symbolized the intangible fruits that "made us strong", "instilled in us our heritage", "safe haven". Not all was rosy as evident in the discrimination and hardships of making a living; but their fortitude and resilience came through. Each found different ways to cope, to learn, and to succeed. All are proud citizens today, having gained support from the community, made it through these hard time, and without the entitlements from government handouts. And "we did it in one generation" as we conclude with Ted Ho's comments.

The stories below highlight what contributed to this resiliency.

Rosemary Lee: We lost everything after crash landing.

Nickname: Rosita
Lived at: Mott St, Chinatown, across Canal Stree
Now Living: Little Neck, NY
Occupation: Nurse
Father's Occupation: Chinese restaurant owner and worker
Mother's Occupation: restaurant worker and beading

of costume jewelry

Biography: I came to the U.S. from Hong Kong in 1956. We were really happy and excited coming to America, going to the Gold Mountain. We bought gifts for our relatives. We made several plane changes to get to Seattle and that's when the plane crashed down to the river. I didn't speak English, none of us did, and it was just terrible—very traumatic. M y two sisters and I shared a pillow which the airline hostess threw to us. We were floating on the water with six hands holding one square pillow. I remember going down to the water, up again, down again, and up again. I swallowed so much water. I thought "I'm gonna die".

We were saved by fishermen in a boat. At that time, I called for God's help. There were two Catholic nuns on the plane; I screamed to them in Chinese for God to save us. In hindsight, it was significant to me because I am a Catholic and I witnessed the two nuns, were so peaceful just floating on the water. We were fighting for the one pillow because we didn't know how to swim. My uncle from NY came to get us after we stayed in the hospital for two or three weeks.

I felt that I was really lucky, although we lost everything. No more gifts for our relatives; nothing, but one sweater, and a pair of pants. So we were very poor. When we came I was very upset. As a teenager, I could hear what people meant. We came to Chinatown for dinner, and were driven to the farm in New Jersey where my father and mother were supposed to be farmers He had a huge house, something I had never seen. However, that night, our relative said to my mother "Look, I'm not happy to see you people. I'm happy because I'm successful and get you here." That meant he didn't really like us. We ended up in New Jersey unable to make long distance calls because my mother was told she would have no money to pay the relative. We could not use their washing machine or dryer because of the electric bill and might break it. My mother had to wash all our clothes by hand in the little bathroom sink. There was no *Gum San* (Gold Mountain)for us here.

Our relatives didn't like us because we had such a big family; three girls and two boys was really bad luck for them. We did not have enough food to eat, just rice. Whenever there was meat, she gave it to her two sons to eat. One day, I felt so upset,. I said to my aunt, "Why don't you teach my mother how to use the washing machine, because it's hard for her to stand there and wash". She snapped at me, "You little girl, shut up!" This was so traumatic and hurtful, and I remember these words to this day. My mother got so scared that I would create a problem that she sent me to Chinatown to live with my grandmother.

I could not go to school for two years and sat home watching King Kong movies. My mother finally found a nun, who had escaped from communist China, to teach me English. My parents finally left the farm and found an 8 story walk up apartment on Broome Street. It was lopsided and had no heat but that was all we could afford. You had to use the kitchen sink to wash up since there was only a tube and a toilet in the bathroom. My parents shared one bedroom; my three sisters shared the other; two of us slept on either end of one twin bunk bed. My two brothers slept on the sofa bed in the living room.

I struggled with minimum English in high school. I always sat way in the back so as not to be noticed or called upon. I was embarrassed when called on. Other students from Hong Kong had learned some English before coming to America; we couldn't afford it. Chemistry changed my life as I saw other girls struggle with the long Latin names as did I, and they spoke English well. When I graduated, I went on to become a Lab Technician. I loved it. I couldn't get a job at first in Manhattan because of discrimination; I ended up in a poor neighborhood in the Bronx. I found it rewarding but then decided I wanted to become a nurse. to help people.

When I met John, I was not so eager to get married. I had taken on the housekeeping chores for my family and siblings, doing the shopping, the cooking. I had to collect my siblings from after school, and make sure they did their homework. I didn't get to do mine till 11PM. As soon as I could get working papers, I did and worked at various jobs to bring in some income. My mother ended up in a sweat shop in Chinatown as a seamstress for 30-40 years. My father went to work as a cook in a restaurant in Ting Yat Sick. He went on to others until he was able to open his own restaurant in Brooklyn. We all worked in the restaurant until we got married. He closed it after that, and bought a two family house in Flushing—achieving the American dream.

My belief in God kept me going. I often had two jobs to earn money. We faced a lot of discrimination in school. People would laugh when I pronounced words wrong, or make funny sounds to mimic the Chinese language. I lived across Canal Street and the Italian boys always made fun of me. I'd hold my head up high and pretend I didn't hear. I also encountered when shopping. Several times when I asked to look at an expensive item, I was questioned as to whether or not I had the money.

Accomplishment: I became a Registered Nurse. Although I didn't recall meeting any Chinese as a R.N in those days at the hospitals or medical labs, I don't think I was the first, second or even third.

I am blessed that my two daughters went to Ivy League schools and became a lawyer and a dentist. I am happy and at peace. My only regret is that I could not help my mother who died of COPD at the age of 72 after a 10 year bout. I could not help her. But as they say, "I never promised you a rose garden." My crash landing immigrating from Hong Kong to the U.S. and my fond memories of Transfiguration Church and dances at the Four Seas and the Vikings stand in contrast.

Lillian Cheu

I- came over on the Empress of China (large ship) from Guangzhou, China, and went through Vancouver, Halifax, and Ellis Island; it took 2 weeks. My father was the son of a citizen, connected to the history of the transcontinental railroad. He came over, owned a Chinese laundry; made it in under the Exclusion Act 1938 as a businessman-laundry. He was Leong by birth; Chin by paper; and kept his Chin name till he married

Bad Boys of Chinatown

Known for hanging out in the pool rooms and Chinatown bars, they came to be known as the *kai doy* (bad boys) of Chinatown. All ended up becoming upstanding American citizens and having productive careers. Daniel Moy, known by his friends as the Mayor of Chinatown, below tells his story.

Daniel Moy: We were the *kai doy*—We wanted to expand our experience.

Nickname: Skinny
Year Born: 1942
Lived at: 56 Mott Street, Chinatown
Now Living: La Habra, California
Occupation: Vice President of Sales
Father's Occupation: Owned Pagoda Chinese restaurant; president of On Leong Ton and the Moy Association
Mother's Occupation: Performer in Barnum Bailey Circus; then a Garment factory worker; costume jewelry beading; and ran the family business Dress shop over 10 years.

Biography: First I like to tell a little story about my mother **Mabel Moy.** She was born in Shanghai in 1919. As the story went, she was sold to a street circus act at the age 6. She later became one of the top performers. In 1936, the troop join Barney Bailey Circus where she traveled all over the world. In 1939, she performed in the New York World's Fair. There were many newspapers clippings which I wished I kept. She did have a young son name Richard. One day, her nanny ran away with the baby. After 3 years, she finally located the son and nanny. Because the boy was so attached to the nanny, she gave up the boy.

This is when I, Skinny Danny, came into the picture. My mom was connected with the Bo Bo restaurant crowd on Pell Street—where mostly Chinese Opera show business people hung out. I loved going there as a kid because there were so many beautiful ladies. My mom was a very hard worker. She did just about everything to help the family make it.

My dad also did just about everything. My dad owned a jewelry store on 52 Mott street; he also owned the Pagoda restaurant which is no longer there. It was a landmark, right dead center Chinatown. We had an interest in Sun Sing Theater. I remember traveling with him to Boston, Chicago, and Washington DC; he was a great speaker, a calligrapher, and well educated.

I know everyone in Chinatown. My father was one of the presidents of *On Leong Tong* (Chinese Merchants Association). He spoke *Kwang Dong Hwa* (Cantonese) and my mom spoke *Joong Kok Hwa* (Mandarin). I knew how to speak *Toisan Hwa* (Toisan dialect) because I lived in Chinatown. I am very proud to be Chinese and I'm one of the people who is actually Chinese first. Cosmetically, I am not.

Experience of the *Kai Doys*: My name is Daniel Moy, they called me Skinny Danny. There's two Danny Moys in Chinatown; one was short and fat and I was skinny. I grew up with my friends in Chinatown; **Larry Lau** lived in the same building on the same floor; **Lungie (Henry Eng)** lived at 56 Mott Street. Growing up, I didn't know that I was adopted so I considered myself as an ugly duckling because I did not look like everyone else—Chinese. I never knew I was half and half (part Chinese and part Polish) and adopted at two weeks until I was 14. I always thought I was different but I never knew the difference. My buddy Lungie was also adopted. My environment in Chinatown was very close as a family, and really supportive.

As I grew up I never knew anything about prejudice because we grew up as a group. I later found out about the prejudice from the *Jook Kock Doys*—the immigrants from China. My Chinese is pretty good but I'm considered *Jook Sing*. I noticed the *Jook Kocks* had a very difficult time adjusting into this country. They had to work in Chinatown, in the Chinese restaurants and sweatshops, wet washes and in the laundries—what anybody did as an immigrant. So I understand the difficulties having lived in Chinatown. I think as the second generation, we the *Jook Sing* opened the doors for the *Jook Kocks*.

I remember working in Chinatown; it was very difficult for us to get outside of Chinatown. We had to think outside the box. And a lot of us did not know how to do that. So we felt uncomfortable. For example, Larry was an artist; when he went to the outside world, he felt a little bit out of place.

So we had to work a little bit harder. That's what I learned from my childhood and my parents; if you work hard, it pays off. My dad always taught me, if you give 110% and you will be successful in life one time or another. When they came over as immigrants, they had it very difficult. They worked in laundries, garment factories.

We grew up in the DuWop era so we wanted to be like James Dean (a famous actor in the 1940s in mainstream America). We grew our hair [long and slicked back] and had motorcycles. [We were into Rock and Roll.] We sure felt that we were on the top of society. Then the Taiwanese group came over here with a silver spoon. They came over here after President Chang Kai Shek (Chinese Nationalist Government in Taiwan), and had money and property. I can give you a story about Madame Chiang Kai Shek. When she came to the U.S. in 1949, she needed support from the Cantonese people. She went to the Chinese Consolidated Benevolent Association where they had Wah Keuh Chinese School for help. The women's group there took this big Chinese flag of Taiwan down Mott Street, and people threw money into the flag to help Madame Chang Kai Shek settle down here. What she did was to buy all the property uptown, which she then sold to the people from northern China. So that's how we had the separation Chinatown between the *Bok Low* (Northerners) and the Cantonese people (i.e., the Uptown-Downtown dichotomy discussed in Chapter 6).

Our group, the *Kai Doys*, grew up and actually did very well. We were the "bad boys". We did everything. Everything that kids who went to school never did. You name it, we did it. We had a lot of fun doing it. But we also remembered that we were taught by our parents about our culture—to get an education, to work hard, and hand off children. That's it. [Asked if he regretted being a bad boy, he said] No, I love it. The reason is being part of the group, not a bad group. We were *special guys*. We just wanted to be outside of the box. We wanted to experience what everyone else did. Everyone went to school but they really did not experience the different cultures. We wanted to be outside the box and we wanted to spread our wings. I think **Baayork Lee** did that as a performer. **Larry Lau** is an artist …. I'm a BS artist (in jest). I'm in Sales. We are very talented people. We also have a lot of people who became doctors and lawyers. Very boring (in jest). But we had fun, I believe. And we spread our wings a little bit better than other people.

I'm a Catholic, I went to Transfiguration Church. I also went to True Light church because they had a beautiful gym. I went to the Mariners Temple because they had a nice gym. The more churches we went to, we found out that we get to meet more ladies. And that's why I went to church.

The Dances by the Jade Club and the Four Seas Club:

Everyone remembers the dances and how it afforded an opportunity for Chinese to meet other Chinese in a safe environment. **Skinny Danny** and a group of his buddies founded the Jade Club, also known as the *Jook Sing* club, that hosted some of the many dances in Chinatown. The *Jook Kock clubs* included the Four Seas and Poy Ching clubs to which many *Jook Sings* also attended. Some held these dances as fundraisers for True Light Church sports teams. The onset of the Chinese youth gangs in the 1960s marked the end of these dances that our participants so fondly cherish to this day. Chinatown became unsafe because these gangs would invade these public community events causing havoc. John Lee, chronicled below, became known as one of the best Lindy dancers.

John Lee: I cleaned myself up!

Lived at: Chinatown
Now living in Little Neck, NY
Nickname: John Jr
Occupation: Realtor

Biography: His father died when he was young. His mother got sick and died after a four year hospitalization. This left John with his two sisters in a 2 room flat in Chinatown. He recalls taking a walk when his sisters took a bath to give them privacy. He slept on the couch in his uncle's living room, grateful just to have a place to sleep He recalls having to work in the restaurants to support his sisters and himself when he was in his teens. After his mother died, he started hanging out in the pool rooms and gambling. He blew away $40,000 that he had saved. With barely a dime in his pocket, he enlisted in the military service, "I cleaned myself up". He came back from the military and avoided the gambling dens and pool rooms. He married, and became a realtor. He raised two daughters, put them through Ivy League colleges; they became attorneys.

To our Parents: The Pioneers

Many are indebted to their parents for the sacrifices they made in coming to America. They acknowledge their hardworking struggle to make it here not for themselves, but for their children to have a better future. Most do not forget their obligation to their parents, and the messages they received which urged them to study hard, be upstanding individuals, and to be loyal to family. There is a term in Chinese for this—shi gu, which does not exist in the English language.

Hard work and Discipline

At the 50s Kick Off Event, one group consisting of: **John Yee, Gloria Lee Yee, Tommy Moy, Lenny Loo, Gingee Moy, Linda Lee, Lehman "Ray" Lee,** (in the picture), and **Susan Doshim, Loretta Lee Chow, Eva Lui, and Rogers Lui** (not in the picture) shared their vivid and fond

memories of growing up in Chinatown. They attributed much of their success to the hard work, discipline and instilling of Chinese values taught to them by their parents.

Gloria Yee recalled that "for those living in 37 Mott Street, we were one big family; it was safe in Chinatown. Hanging out, running across the tenement rooftops, playing childhood games of stickball, Johnny on the pony, trading baseball cards, and no TV are memories we all miss [compared with] the overload of videogames these days. Those who did not live in Chinatown remembered coming into Chinatown on Sundays for groceries, **getting** fresh killed chicken, having dinner, and socializing. A typical scenario included parents going to the *fong or* the family clan association as a weekly ritual to play mahjong, and socialize with members. For the "kids", this group recalled fond memories of going out to play at the arcade, Columbus Park, and stick ball. The family all met for dinner and went home.

Hardworking Parents: The majority of the parents were in the laundry business; the family often lived in the back of the laundry with only a few rooms or 1 bedroom for families of 5-7. All had the incentive to get an education so they could get out of the laundry. All went on to professions outside the laundry with the encouragement of their parents. As **Gingee**

Moy said, you "just had to see how hard they worked 6 ½ days a week; as kids, we had to help out with the ironing of handkerchiefs and shirt sleeves, and we knew we did not want to stay in the laundry". The exceptions were notable. **Susan Doshim**'s father owned the first Chinatown Pharmacy; **Lenny Loo**'s father owned a wet wash, the wholesale side of the laundry business. **Ray Lee**'s father was a college professor in China, but became a laundry owner in the U.S. because there was no opportunity to use his skills here.

Discipline from our parents: The group recalled the following quotes from their parents when being disciplined. *Ah sei nei* (i.e., I'll beat you to death) used as a threat to indicate the seriousness of the infraction (**Loretta Lee Chow**). "Don't do anything that will make me ashamed of you" (**Ray Lee**) with an emphasis on the importance of *face* in the Chinese culture. **Gingee Moy** use an example to demonstrate the principle of ethics by her parents. "They made me return some plants I had taken from a neighbor. And then, they gave the neighbor free laundry service for a while to make amends". Memories of the strict parental discipline ranged from "My mother was the disciplinarian and she didn't have to say anything. She looked at us and we knew what we were supposed to do (**Linda Lee**) to "mine used a stick" (**Eva Lui**). Parental discipline focused on working hard, getting an education, and respecting seniority and loyalty to the family. **John Yee**'s parents "were seldom around because they were [too busy] working; when they were, they would say, keep your nose to the books and keep studying because you gotta do better than that". **Gingee Moy**'s recalls being strictly disciplined for not calling her older sister by *Ah Dee* (i.e., older sister) and was made to stand in the corner for hours. As **Lenny Loo** said, "we were raised 75% by ourselves because they were always working". In the end, however, **Lenny Loo** described his father "as a-quiet man, but you can see the special glow in his eyes when someone did something right and it was good for the family. I wish every son could see that [from his father]."

Discrimination: Although none talked about daily discrimination (which may have been a function of where they lived), most talked about incidents where they were made fun of by name calling, others making faces to mimic Chinese eyes, and to physical violence—someone throwing rocks at her sister which required stitches or someone trying to beat you up after school. Many remembered being considered the smart Asian kid where others wanted to copy their answers in class.

Lily Ho: It is more important to tell our parents' stories.

Lily Ho, wife of Ted Ho for more than 50 years shares these memories. She lost her parents by the time she was 15, leaving her to take care of her 6 year old brother. She says, "When I was young I knew that I was not going

to a college. Girls were not to go to college, especially if you were laundry or restaurant people. Because I lost my parents, I did not have any dreams. I just accepted things as they were, and did what I had to do." This philosophy carried her through her experiences of discrimination and struggle.

I think these oral history interviews are really good, but it is based on our history and stories. I think it is more important to tell our parents' stories. How did they get here? How did they manage with so little care? What did they have to do? Not everybody knows the history of their family because years ago, people came in illegally. No one was going to talk about that but they're gone now.

James Y.K. Moy: "We were raised basically in "fatherless" homes.

Nickname: Gan
Year Born: 1934
Lived at: 37 Mott Street; 44 Mulberry Street, Chinatown
Occupation: Minister; Vice President of Student Affairs, Wartburg College
Father's Occupation: Chinese restaurant owner in Brooklyn
Mother's Occupation: Beading of costume jewelry and babysat for young mothers who worked in garment factories.
Biography: We were raised basically in "fatherless" homes. My father worked 10-12 hrs. a day, seven days a week; he'd hang out at the restaurant even on his days off and help out during the rush hours! The only fathers I knew were the working ones right in Chinatown!

I won the Music Medal on graduation from PS130. I joined the Chinatown Basketball Club on Elizabeth Street as a teenager with the *Clowns*; I was a Cub Scout/Boy Scout Troop 150 and played softball; I was in the Drum and Bugle Corp in Chinese School, in the True Light Church Choir, Modern Dance and Ballet, Violin and Piano. I have a B.A in Biology and History from Valparaiso University; a Masters of Divinity from Lutheran Theological Seminary, Gettysburg, PA.; MA in Guidance and Counseling, Teachers College, and PhD in Guidance and Counseling, Ohio University.

Accomplishment: Recipient of the First Bush Leadership Fellowship Award, given by the Bush Foundation of Minnesota. There were four of us in the first class which started in 1966. I was the first Chinese American recipient. I was also the first Chinese American recipient of Valparaiso University's Outstanding Alumni Award for Professional Achievement 1989. There were three Multicultural Leaders Ordained in the United Lutheran Church of America in 1960. I was the first Chinese American from within the ULCA who was ordained then. I was very proud of being elected Vice President of the Student Body at Valparaiso in my Junior year!

Fondest memories: Chinatown Field Day at Columbus Park in the summers. Playing Handball against the wall on Mott Street by *Wah Kueh* Chinese School before classes began. Visiting with friends in their apartments in Chinatown. Watching the Priests praying at Transfiguration Church from the rooftop of 37 Mott Street. Eating *Sam Jup Mein* in Chinatown; Dim Sum at Lee's after church; 75 Cent haircuts on Doyers Street, meeting friends at the Chinatown Fair and at *Nom Wah Parlor*. Hanging around outside of 37 Mott Street, and listening to the "older" folk teasing and joking with one another.

Growing experience: Yes, there is a success story; but the questions of resiliency and strength do not touch on the emotional turmoil in an environment with conflicting cultural values, family conflicts, and the social isolation I experienced while growing up. That I was able to overcome them was largely due to patient, loving people at my church, later on at Valparaiso University and Teachers College where I had caring professors who understood the problems and conflicts of "marginality" experienced by the youth in this country. "Telling My Story" has been therapeutic, but it was done in Sociology and Psychology classes and in graduate school where we wrote "logs" describing our family relationships. I am grateful to the doctoral graduate who read my logs and offered invaluable insights to help me understand where I have been and who I have become. I shared those logs with a Chinese student in one of my graduate classes and his response was telling—he said, "This sounds like my story as well."

Ray Lee: My father was a college professor in China

Year Born: 1942
Lived at: Harlem, NY
Occupation: Printer
Father's Occupation: Laundry
Biography: My father came over to this country; he was a college professor in China. So when he came over here, there

was no job for him in the colleges to teach….to teach Chinese language? He couldn't speak the language, so he ended up opening up a laundry. Initially, he was a merchant, and traveled a lot to Cuba to trade materials before coming over here. Then he went back to China, and brought my mother to the U.S. We lived in a laundry. There was five children, with two adults. So there was seven of us living in the back of the laundry, from my childhood to teenage years. We were on our own after that.

Fondest memories: My fondest memories of growing up in Chinatown were going to Chinese school. I ended up a lot of the times in the principal's office where he broke a lot of rulers on the palm of my hand. He couldn't wait till I quit, which I did. I joined the Chinese School Drum and Bugle Corp and spent a lot of time with a lot of the friends I met in Chinatown—in the pool room, the penny arcade, and the poker games down by the courthouse. The cops would join us in these games too—they never arrested us.

Dottie Chin: My mother was the first Chinese female funeral director

Lived in: Mulberry Street, Chinatown
Occupation: Nurse
Mother's Occupation: Wah Wing Sang Funeral Home Director
Biography: Came at the age of 10 to Chinatown from Philadelphia; lived on Mulberry St above the mortuary; attended P.S. 23; went to Bradley Beach
Fondest Memories: the celebrations during Chinese New Year; the Lion's dance especially at night; the colors were wonderful. My

primary group was True Light Church; played basketball with the Royals; it was a very special era;
Mother's Biography: Martha Yick was my mother; she was a business woman; the first Chinese female funeral director of the Wah Wing Sang Funeral Home. We lived above the mortuary; there were only three Chinese funeral home in all of the East Coast, and they were all located on one block on Mulberry Street. My eventually expanded by buying out the one next door. My mother and stepfather started the business. He had a good business mind while she was proficient in Chinese. When my stepfather dropped out of the picture; my mother continued to operate the business. My brother later joined business and I worked there too at one point.

My mother was my role model. Everyone remembers her as Aunt

Martha; she was a real people person. She was generous, kind hearted, and always willing to help others in any way she could. She would help widows with their social security. She helped families go through their grieving, and help them go through the bridges they had to cross when arranging a funeral for their loved ones. She appreciated tradition and treated the families and their loved ones with the respect they deserved. Lots of people don't like associating with the funeral business; people would cross the street to avoid having to walk passed the funeral home. My mother was well known in the community; she was active in True Light Church, the Ladies Guild, the Chinese American Legion, and with many of the charities. She immersed herself in it and loved what she was doing to help others.

She was born in San Francisco, but spoke excellent Chinese and was immersed in the Chinese culture and traditions. In fact, she thought in Chinese more than English. She retired after 40+ years and moved to San Francisco with her second husband. She's in her 90s now and remains very active in the community. Her message to people would be: Be generous with those you know and love, and it always come back to you.

Our Social Networks Made Us Strong

Chinese values and Identity

At the 50s Kick Off Event, another group talked of their Chinese heritage and Chinese values which made them strong, and proud to be Chinese. Many in this group grew up in the back of the Chinese hand laundry. **Daniel Moy, Park Gong, Ed Chin, and Henry Hum** came from families with Chinese hand laundries. Many lived in the back of these laundries. **Park Gong** says, "it was no fun". They often did not tell their friends although they claimed not to be embarrassed by it. **Marjorie Chung Davis** says, "though I was embarrassed and never told my friends as a child, today, I wear it as a badge of honor", a tribute to my Chinese heritage.

Daniel K. Moy: It was our heritage!

Lived: Astoria, NY
Parents' Occupation: Chinese hand laundry
Occupation: Senior Director, Computer Operations, NYC Department of Education
Descriptive Quote: It was the heritage; hanging out with my buddies from Brooklyn Tech; our Chinese heritage was instilled in me. We have to continue it.

Biography: I grew in Astoria, NY. My parents would come to Chinatown every Sunday. If I didn't hang out with my Brooklyn Tech buddies, I would have been hanging out with others, and lost my Chinese heritage. I would have hung out with the Greeks and the Italians who were in my neighborhood. That would have been fine, but I would have lost being Chinese, and that's important to me

I moved to Queens with my parents when I was 5 years old. From 5 to next 10 years, we'd always come to Chinatown to do the normal Sunday thing. We'd pick up groceries, meet on the street corners, meet aunts and uncles in Chinatown, *yum cha*. It really started in high school, at Brooklyn Tech when I was 15 or 16. We started to get together with Chinese friends; then, we'd get together with Chinese women. We started to hang out in Chinatown, right in front of Lonnie's Coffee Shop, never inside, every Sunday for another four or 5 years. I wouldn't miss it for anything; it was great. There were the social gatherings and Transfiguration Church. Then, there were the bars—Yuks, Nona, Grandpa's; and Lucy Jung's; you'd go there at nights for socialization.

We lived in the back of the laundry; I used to hang out with friends at their houses. When they would ask to come over to my place, I'd say, No, no, no. They used to meet me in front of the laundry, but they never knew we lived in the back. It gave me strength. To tell the truth, people kidded me because I was Chinese. Coming here to Chinatown, I became proud I was Chinese. Realistically, I got kidded as kid a lot about being Chinese; but here, Chinese are strong; it was the support mechanism in Chinatown; they gave it to me. The typical Chinese kid was meek and quiet; coming to Chinatown gave me the opportunity to learn; it gave me the strength, not so much to fight back, but to be supported, and to be more aggressive.

Ours is a story we just have to communicate to the younger generation; my nieces and nephews don't understand this; they're not into Chinese heritage; they have Chinese friends; but they're just friends. I was never embarrassed by my laundry origins. In fact, I was one of the Chinese activists at Columbia University—went there during the days of the riots. . I had the long hair; was not shy. Then, I went into business and got conservative again.

Ed Chin: Our Confucian Values

Lived at: little Italy, NY
Occupation: Physician
Descriptive Quote: I owe my being to my life experiences. My richest experience was

in Chinatown. The next is education; its value is engrained in the Chinese culture. A main precept of Confucian values is our respect for the scholar. According to Confucian analects, it is written that the scholar is the highest; it is not the merchant, not the solider, not the businessman. This carried down from the emperor to the peasantry.

Biography: I grew up in little Italy; it was adjacent to Chinatown then; it's become Chinatown now. I lived near the park by Bowery Savings Bank. I went to Columbia University and then on to medical school to become a physician.

Park Gong: Living in the back of the laundry was no fun.

Lived: Harlem and moved to Baxter St, Chinatown

Parents Occupation: Laundry

Biography: I grew up in a Chinese laundry; I lived in the back of the laundry at 141 St and Lenox Ave during grades 1 to 3 at St Mark's Catholic School. I used to be a bad boy, used to always get the ruler. We moved to Chinatown when I was in 4th grade to Baxter Street across from Fellini's.....Chinatown was OK, no different from Harlem; it was an experience. Then I went to New York University.

Living in the back of the Chinese laundry was no fun. We went to Chinatown on Sundays for supplies. My parents would buy me a comic book or two, and I was happy. A truck from Chinatown would come up to Harlem every week carrying Chinese food; then; there was the fish man, and the watermelon man selling watermelons for a dollar; those were the good old days. I used to go back to the laundry to help my father out.

Henry Hum: Go to a college where 50% are Asian

Experience: My resiliency came from the support of Chinese friends and community success. My friends and I used to meet in front of the laundry; and we'd play in front of the laundry, but I never told then I lived there.

Later, I came to Chinatown for the social activities—football, baseball. My Chinese School experience was a joke. I was in 1st grade for 2 years; I finally got promoted to 2nd grade and then they sent me back to 1ˢᵗ grade. Then I met Joey, my cousin Jimmy, and we'd hang out at Lonnie's Coffee Shop; it was the only American place. We'd all go over there; it was the corner where everyone met. We went to Chinese dances on weekends, the bowling alley; we went to eat. Did that for 5 or 6 years; it was the way we grew up; the way to meet Chinese friends. Today, there aren't those opportunities. There is not a place to go meet Chinese friends. For example, what is the ratio of Chinese in colleges today? 2%?; then, Chinese shouldn't go there. You've; gotta go to a college where 50% are Asian; we have to get our children to go there; but, it's a different world today.

Margie Chung Davis: : What's a girl like me from Harlem doing in Chinatown?

Lived at: Harlem, NY; 149 St and Broadway
Now living: upstate New York
Occupation: Real Estate
Father's Occupation: Laundry
Unique experience: A lot of my fond memories are with my dad around the kitchen table in the back of the laundry. Our Chinese hand laundry was on 149th and Broadway in Harlem. My grandfather was the first to come over with my granduncle.

So what's a girl like me from Harlem doing in Chinatown? My sisters dragged me out to Chinatown when I was young. I was 13 years old; they put make up on me, fishnet stockings, and dragged me out to the dances. I remember meeting Chinese people for the first time, going to dances.   There was not a lot of Chinese up in my neighborhood; I remember going to Lonnie's Coffee Shop on Mott Street; the lime rickeys, egg creams; and hamburgers for 25 or 30 cents. I had my own network of friends I played basketball on an all girl's Chinese team. It makes me feel so grounded; so many with the same roots. Chinatown provided the support and made me proud that I was Asian. Growing up, I was a real minority in my neighborhood. I was picked on a lot when I was little.   When I came down to Chinatown, I was part of the whole community. I feel a certain strength. After all these years, I still come seeking my Asian friends, and arranging socials; feeling strong.

I'm so proud of my grandfather; he came to US with very little English. He built a business that thrived. He brought all the relatives over. I'm sorry that our kids don't have the same work ethic that we had. Today, when you ask then to do something; they're so spoiled.

Growing up in the laundry prepared me for life; I worked at an early age. At 6 years old, I was stamping laundry tickets, wrapping shirts in the brown paper packages. I've seen a lot of adversity, and learned a lot about dealing with business. I was embarrassed living in back of laundry; I never told my friends. I got picked on in school; never wanted to tell; now I wear it as a badge of honor.

Harry Woo: Chinatown gave me culture!!!

Nickname: Moon Head
Lived at: 32 Henry Street, Chinatown
Occupation: Professor of nursing
Father's Occupation: Owned seven Chinese restaurants
Mother's Occupation: Beading of costume jewelry
Accomplishments: I was able to attend college by working as a security guard for Pinkerton Securities at 80 wall street locked in a vault with billions of stock securities. I always worked two jobs, teaching biology at Lincoln high school and working as a waiter in New Jersey or driving a taxi to support my family.

I hold 8 state teaching licenses. I have a BS in biology, MS in political science, PhD in Econometrics and sociology; I graduated magna cum laude. I became the first Chinese truant officer in NYC. I owned three stores in Chinatown—fruit store, fish store, and Kung Foo Martial Arts store, all on Canal Street. I am now teaching *Jook Kocks,* doctors from mainland China, to become nurses. My life has always been to help educate people regardless of their affiliation—whether they are gang members or lost souls from China.

My daughter became a surgeon at age 23; my older daughter became a school psychologist. My adopted son is an aeronautical engineer and is with a missile system protecting this entire country. My son in law Joe is a surgeon at Harvard. My other son in law is a chief at Yale in radiology.
Memories: Fighting the Italians who were picking on the Chinese; and studying in Chinese school for 6 years to be number one so my parents would be proud. My father made me a cook at ten years of age; I was able to use his encouragement to help others. My message is to study hard so white people will respect you; always love and respect your parents.

Harold and Ronald Lui:

Harold and Ronald Lui, brothers, discuss growing up in Chinatown, their involvement with sports, basketball, and the True Light Church. "We were introduced to American life through our affiliation with True Light Church. The church was phenomenal; it was our moral foundation and taught us the values of life." Their father died when they were about 9 and 10 years old leaving their mother alone to raise 8 children. Relatives from their village, were major sources of support and help with the uncles providing a father figure in their lives. Their family owned restaurant hired relatives, provided them with a strong sense of community within the extended family network and provided them with their first jobs—making for their resiliency and strength in dealing with the outside world.

Quote: I am most proud that we were part of an identity that the community went through. We opened the road, and paved the way for Chinese to become an integral part of the society—the way they should be.

Harold's Biography: Harold, born in 1934, was nicknamed Cheesy. He was Executive Director of the Chinatown Health Center for more than a decade (now the Wang Community Health Center). He is proud of his social work background, because he loved basketball so much, he used these skills to teach and help youth from Chinatown. He organized teams and coached basketball during the 50s, and intervened during the gang problem of violence and extortion in the 60s, risking his life and career for this cause.

Accomplishments: Harold helped to found the Chinatown Planning Council, one of the first social services agency in Chinatown, and was responsible for helping to organize these services as one of the first, and few, Chinese speaking social workers in NYC. "We brought together the social workers and health providers in Chinatown—all wanting to help [because there were no social services then]; all the other [social service] organizations in Chinatown grew from that period of time." Too much to chronicle here, they did a nice job of raising money for the summer youth program, the Head Start program which is the forerunner of all the CPC day care centers today, counseling and health services. "That was amazing in 1965-66; it just grew and grew".

Quote: It is balance: adapting to the outside world while maintaining our Chinese culture

Year Born: Ronald 1933

Father's Occupation: Managed Hop Kee Restaurant on 21 Mott Street; formerly Ting Yit Sick

Ronald's Biography: We first lived on Christie St, and moved to Park St (now Mosco St, Chinatown. We developed a formula where everyone who worked put money into the kitty to pay for the expenses—groceries, etc. The system worked, and we were able to buy a house

and move to Woodside, Queens, but we still came down to Chinatown. We call it our home. We all had pretty much the same background in Chinatown—immigrant families. I got drafted into the army after high school. Because of the GI bill after the Korean War in the 70s, I finished college, married and raised a family. We both took advantage and made good use of the public services—free public education for high school and college.

The brothers recall the kerosene and ice they were responsible for to bring into the house to heat the stove in the winter, and to cool the icebox. "We had to go out in the streets to wait for the truck to come by, and buy 5 gallons at a time…We'd go up 2 flights of stairs, open up the heater and pour it in. The boys were only ones who were strong enough to do this. We slept with the kerosene stove on [dangerous to do]. We risked our lives every winter. When our kids now complain about air conditioning or the heat, I'd say 'You guys don't know what you are missing'." The heat was only from the stove in the kitchen. When it got really cold, we put newspapers around the windows to keep out the draft, or underneath our clothes to keep warm. We took cold water baths, once a week because you heated your own hot water. We used the kitchen sink to wash clothes and brush our teeth; it was the only sink.

Fondest Memories: Their story was a joint interview with rich detail—too much to present in this brief bio. The following are highlights. There were 8 of us in the family. We had four brothers and always had company playing with one another; we made up our own games. My father used to work long hours with two different jobs. He had a stroke and died in 1943. My mother was a single parent, but we had a lot of help from relatives and the minister who lived next door. My mother was a very positive and highly moral person. She had two vices; she smoked, and played mahjong a lot. Some of the words she used were pretty foul but I didn't know what they meant back then.

We didn't have much, but then we didn't expect much. My mother never wanted anything from anyone. She was willing to work hard. We did not have much space, just enough to get into our beds; we had 8 in one room and 4 in another. We never noticed it.

They have fond memories of Christmas at True Light Church with the candlelight service, the pageant, learning the Christmas story, and all the donated toys, brightly wrapped set up on the piano. There were the dances at True Light with the fox trot, lindy, and a little Latin music. We later sponsored them for fundraising. After the basketball games, the boys had to run to take a quick shower before the dance. The whole world is different now; we don't even try to explain it to our kids.

There was the Chinese newspaper industry back then Kids would make money selling newspapers for 3 or 4 cents on the street. Our friends worked there at the printing presses to get them in the mail 6 days a week to places like Philadelphia, Boston, and the laundries in the outer boroughs. (This was often the only news the Chinese immigrants received.)

The brothers taught Sunday school at True Light Church trying to provide positive role models to the youth in the 50s. When the Chinese gangs came into Chinatown in the 60s, hey would hear about the physical violence, recruitment by the gangs of junior high school kids, extortion and corruption; "that's when the fireworks stopped in Chinatown".

The brothers shared a job in a restaurant to help the family make ends meet. "We worked 28 hours a weekend on Saturday and Sunday. We washed the tea-cups, the dishes, peeled the shrimps, and dried the dishes. My other brothers worked at another restaurant—7 hours a day on Friday and Saturday night till 2 o'clock in the morning. Restaurants were open 24 hours in those days. So if you really wanted to make money, you could make money. We bought a house based on the formula we used to contribute to the household expenses; it kept us all together; we buy our cars, we share our cars.

Every Chinese New Year, my mother would cook Chinese New Year (pastries) for everyone; it was great. The uncles, restaurant workers from the family business, family and relatives would also come to get them. When they gave *hung bow* (red envelopes), they had to give 8 envelopes [because we had 8 kids]. And they were generous. I have a great sense of family and community from this that I will never forget to this day. No one will ever take that away from me. People today don't do it anymore. Our friends don't care about it. They just never got the full meaning of Chinese New Year.

Proudest moments: For Harold, I just think that we were part of an identity that the community went through. We opened the road, and paved the way for Chinese to become an integral part of the society in a way they should be. It allowed us to really make use of whatever we came with— intelligence, culture—to create a way of life that is healthy and good. I think that was my greatest accomplishment....We did not give up what we learned from the community and what we did when we were kids. Because of us, we did all these big things.

There were number of history projects going way back to the time of the Vietnam war starting with the Basement Workshop, which became the Chinatown history museum, and now MOCA. Harold was on the board and contributed to the Lui family collection. The most famous was a picture of my two sisters with hands on their chest singing a church song about Jesus (they called it a pledge of allegiance though). They even put that picture on a metro card.

Impact of growing up in Chinatown: To Harold, the values I learned was the main thing. Nothing else ever taught me how to really adapt to the outside world. It was to achieve a proper balance between the Chinese culture and what's outside in "the other world".

For Ronald, it was the value of keeping the Chinese customs. I have all American friends who don't know too much about Chinese culture. Being brought up in Chinatown, we saw the Chinese customs, they were reinforced. I love the Chinese customs. You want to teach it to your kids, but I don't know if I've been that successful. Only in Chinatown when you meet the old relatives, can you talk and relate to these customs.

Harold and Ronald always go back to Chinatown. When my brother Ronald's mother-in-law died, "Where do you think we had the funeral? In Chinatown". We still go there to shop, but I don't see many people who I know still living there. My accountant and my lawyer are all still there. I don't depend on Chinatown for the services, but anything Chinese, we depend on the Chinese food, the Chinese groceries. Chinatown was a part of our entire life; the Chinese part of it, and a strong part of it. It continues to be the basis for the way of thinking and doing things—and reflects a real understanding and meaning of Confucius.

No Entitlements along the Way

As **Daniel Lee** said, we worked hard, "and we received no entitlements along the way. This sentiment was emphasized repeatedly by the contributors.

Lai Chu: You see I'm a fighter....And as a community, we did not go on welfare.

Year Born: 1942
Lived at: 85 Mulberry Street, Chinatown
Occupation: Community Organizer
Family business: Shing On grocery store
Father's Occupation: Owner of a grocery store in Chinatown
Mother's Occupation: Garment factory worker, Beading of costume jewelry
Fondest memory: Chinatown was a small "community" and sort of had a "closed protected" environment whereby one makes friends easily. You knew "who" everyone was and where everyone lived...it was a simpler world then!
Growing Experience: Living in Chinatown in the 50's and 60's was interesting in that the discrimination we talk so much about did not seem to "affect" or "hamper" our existence. Perhaps we were naive or it did not matter.....we just moved on! Fast forward to today, 60 years later, I believe we, our generation are successful and accomplished contributors to our

society.

The only problem I had was I couldn't speak English. And I was put into a grade 3 at 9 years old. That's when I experienced discrimination. People laughed at you because why would a 9 year old not speak English? In those days, there were a lot of Chinese students at P.S. 23 but there was also a mix of Italians. I would come home and cry because the kids would make fun of me. What saving me was I went to Chinese school.

The discrimination that I experience was more from the Chinese, what the culture imposed on me as a woman. I had two brothers and my parents always said, because funds are limited, they felt that the sons should get the education, not the daughters. They did not have a college education. ....You see I'm a fighter. I met my future husband, and said I'm going to marry him. He was from Toronto, and I told my parents that I'm going to move (in 1967). They opposed; they didn't want me to leave. Their values were that the sons get the education, and the daughters go to high school, get a secretarial job, and get married at 17 or 18. I did not subscribe to any of that. So I had to fight the whole damned system. Not only did I fight my own family and culture; I also had to fight the big system in order to move ahead with my life.

But it all worked out for me. When I married my husband, he's Chinese by his culture but he's not Chinese from his point of view. I became even more independent. When my kids were young, he encouraged me to go back to the university. I got my degree in psychology and sociology while my kids were young. From then on, I was able to grow into the person I became.

Accomplishment: I have been living in Toronto for 47 years and became a real activist there. I am one of the board directors for a large non-profit for 30 something years, and was involved politically. I am know as "she gets you into trouble". I am very active in my community. The attitude there is that if you live in a community, you have to participate and do things that benefit your community. Everyone needs to be engaged. But what's important is I'm willing to be the chair; I step up to the plate. However, I recognized that you need other people to support you. You have to contribute to your community or your society; if everybody comes together to do that, it is so much easier—you can move a mountain.

Lai (Chow?)
1956

Lai's cousin, **Elvin Wingay,** sings her praises. Lai and her family immigrated to NYC in the early 1950s and were among those "downtown Chinese" before she moved to Toronto and married my cousin. This past year, she was recognized for her continuous contribution to the community by being awarded Senior of the Year for the municipality of Toronto by the Province of Ontario. This is but one of many such awards with which she has been honored over the years....At the end of the day, people of Chinese descent have made contributions and have achieved high levels of success in all walks of life—all from humble beginnings from a three-story walk up on Mulberry Street and income derived from the sweatshops and the sale of Chinese dry goods. Entrepreneurship, intestinal fortitude, sacrifice, determination, stubbornness, vision, sense of community and strong family values were the currencies that the "downtown Chinese", like Lai and her family, parlayed into making a life for the family and a future for her children and generations to follow.

Resiliency: My experience of being "discriminated" against as a woman by my Chinese culture impacted my view of " justice " about how people are treated. When I married my Chinese Canadian husband, Gilbert's upbringing and attitudes, value system, encouragement and support have allowed me to do what I do in Toronto. His father was the first Asian male medical doctor to graduate from University of Toronto's medical school in 1925. I have been a "community activist" for the last 35 years...always "fighting" for a good cause and for my community.

My spirit is echoed in the Chinatown community; we did not go on welfare or benefit from any government entitlements along the way. This sentiment was echoed by **Mary Sit**, another of the contributors to this book, whose father owned Wo Ping restaurant. As she says, "Even though our parents may have entered the country without proper papers, we were mindful that we never had any government help".

Marion Chin (Wu): My mother told me: Don't embarrass the family by misbehaving

Year Born: 1933
Lived at: 174 Canal Street, Chinatown
Live now in: Bayside, NY
Occupation: Nurse
Father's Occupation: Chinese restaurant worker
Mother's Occupation: Chinese School teacher at Transfiguration and True Light Chinese Schools
Biography: Marion came from a family of four girls who were all college graduates. The importance of education was emphasized. She finished six years of Chinese school, graduated from Hunter College as a Chemistry major, from Case Western Reserve in Nursing, and Long Island University with an MS in Education. She worked in Chinatown as a School Nurse and Public Health Nurse; she was Director of a Family Planning Clinic in Chinatown. She is married to Gordon Chin for almost 53 years with four

children, and remains active in a Bayside Christian Church and a seniors group in Chinatown Baptist Church. Being fluent in Cantonese and as a member of the Chinese community, I have been able to use my nursing background to help many of the newly-arrived immigrants from Hong Kong, Vietnam and China.

Fondest memory: We were a community of families with close ties to each other through church, family and social associations. Growing up, we got to know almost all the people in the community. Our families worked hard and were self-sufficient. It was shameful to be on welfare and rely on the government. As children, we were taught not to embarrass the family by misbehaving.

10 EXTRAORDINARY ACCOMPLISHMENTS OF ORDINARY PEOPLE

The contributors to this book were not Nobel prize winners or presidents, though there were some. They were ordinary citizens and people who made extraordinary accomplishments. Their stories are but the beginning to illustrate the commonalities among this Chinese American community as well as the differences, and what brought them together. Here we look at what happened to them. Though the riches of family, friends and community are not quantifiable, this was the biggest accomplishment of all who spoke of their children and grandchildren, friends and community that bore them riches. **Daniel Lee** creates for us here a family tree of those from NYC's Chinatown. From such a small community, we produced such a huge array of successes. And there are many more. Our stories here highlight only a few.

A Professional Family Tree of those from NYC Chinatown by Daniel Lee

Newton Chin, Tom Moshang, Chester Chin, Ted Ning Jr, Jeanette Moy, Roy Chu, Kenneth Eng, James Ling, Lucille Lew, Jonathan Ligh, Ming Wong...etc..who are **physicians and surgeons**

Henry Woo, Paul Chu, James Quan, Naitan Chu... etc…who are dentists.

Ray Chin, Bruce Chin, Mabel Moy, Arthur Chu, Bob Chin, Ben Tuan, Ken Chow, Vincent Lee Joann Lee, Jean Lau Chin, James Moy, Calvin Lee, Harry Woo, Hung H. Wu, Soon H. Leong...etc. who are **PhD's. in their professional fields of expertise.**

Stanley Chin, Richard Wong, David Moy, Arthur Soong, Therese Liu, Ben Gim, Ed Hong, Gene Chu, Calvin Lee, Irving Chin, William Ng

King...etc...who are **attorneys.**

James Wu, David Leung, Nancy Ng, George Lai, Donald Seetoo, Robert Yan...etc...who are **certified public accountants.**

John Chin, Albert Leong, Marshall Lee, Richard Lee, Kai Wong, Edward Lee, Sing Chu, Al Ko, Daniel Lee... etc. who are **licensed professional engineers.**

Roland Dick, David Eng, James Wong, Douglas Tuan, Ben Tomm... etc...who are **licensed architects**.

Joe Wong, Soy Chu, Ronald Lee, Ernie Mar, Allen Lee, Milton Gee, Richard Mah, Kenneth Lee, Danny Moy, Jean Lee, Ted Ng, Howard Louie, Tom Low...etc...who are **successful entrepreneurs**.

Ronald Tung, Alfred Lee, Peter Leung, Henry Kee, Bill Won...etc...who are **successful bankers.**

Simon Chu, Henry Kee, Peter Chin, Richard Lee, Daniel Lee...etc—who are **corporate executives.**

Clement Lee, David Fletcher, James Moy, Douglas Ong, Joseph Wong...etc...who are Th.D's. or PhD's. in the **ministry.**

Tim Chin, James Ong, Henry Wong, Fred Ng, Eugene Eng, Joe Wong, Philip Eng, Donald Chu, James Chin...etc.. who are successful in **commercial arts, advertising, and related media professions.**

Henry Chin, Willie Wing, John Lee, Seymour Lee, Willie Ng, Ted Jung, Harry Chin, Alfonse Wong...etc. who successfully worked for **Wall Street brokerage firms.**

Richard Chu, Ronald Leung, Guy Chu, Daniel Moy... etc... who are **licensed pharmacists**.

Calvin Lee was Chancellor, University of Maryland; Academic Dean, Boston University; James Moy was Vice President of Student Affairs, Wartburg College; Jean Lau Chin was Academic Dean at Alliant International University and Adelphi University—**administration in higher education.**

Allen Chin, who is a mechanical engineer by profession, was elected Mayor of Westfield, New Jersey; Gene Woo, who is an engineer by profession and was Mayor of Plandome, New York—**engineers to politics.**

Helen Chin, Gingee Moy, JeanMarie Chin, Lila Chu, Elsie Chan, John K. Lee—teachers who became **principals and superintendent in education.**

The list can go on and on......especially, the large number of us that went onto engineering, science, mathematics, and education where we would fill up several pages including as an example: Bob Yun, Jum Chin, Wan Leung, Gim Lee, Jimmy Ng, and Phil Jung at IBM up in the Hudson Valley of New York.

Highlights

Baayork Lee: Getting Out and Giving Back

Occupation: Performing Arts; Director, National Asian Artist Project

Parents Occupation: owner of Wo Hop restaurant

Lived in: Chinatown

Biography: I'm Baayork, yes, meaning precious jewel or precious jade. My mother put an R in my name to make it American. At the age of 5, the casting people from the King and I with Yul Brynner came to Chinatown looking for children to cast in the show. So we all went up to Broadway and I was the only one that got the job! At age 5, I was on Broadway.

I retained my roots in Chinatown. My father was one of the founders of the Wo Hop restaurant in 17th Mott street. I grew up going to Transfiguration School and then having lunch in the restaurant. But I always wanted to be in show business. So after I completed the King and I at the age of 8, I enrolled in Balanchine School for ballet. After school, I would immediately go to my dancing school. But, I still hung around with all the girls at lunch in Chinatown.

But I pursued a career outside of Chinatown in the Broadway musicals. If I had stayed in Chinatown, I would be waiting tables, doing the cash register at the restaurant because usually you went into your family's business. My brothers had to go to the restaurant and wash dishes every Saturday and Sunday because there were no dishwashing machines. I wanted my career outside. But it's funny now because after all these years, I now started an afterschool musical theatre program for kids called Theatre Club at P.S. 124 on Division Street in Chinatown. I also started a company called National Asian Artist Project to help Asian performances, professionals as well as amateurs, to perform in roles that they would never have otherwise be cast as. For the past three years, I produced Oklahoma, Carousal, and this week I'm doing Hello Dolly. It's all off Broadway on 42nd street. I auditioned kids for the King and I and took 14 kids on tour for one year all over the country. Of course we had tutors to go with them and parents. But they got the kind of experience they would never have had— to see the entire USA before they were 11 years old. My mission now is to go back to my community and bring my theatre experience to them.

Eugene Lee: One of the first Chinese police officers in New York City

Year Born: 1941
Lived at: Bayard Street, Chinatown
Now living in: Las Vegas
Occupation: Gold Shield detective for NY Police Department
Father's Occupation: Restaurant
Biography: My great great grandfather came to the U.S. in 1859. I'm a New York Chinatown boy who never left Chinatown until I went to Haaren High School on 59th Street. I'm proud to be Chinese, but when we went to China four years ago, there was no connection. My connections are in Chinatown. My fond memories are of playing basketball, handball, punchball, kick the can—things that kids these days don't do; they're always on their IPads.

After returning from military service, I became a police officer in 1966. I was second to Johnny Kai who was one of the first Chinese detectives back then. I was initially assigned to the Bronx; they never saw a Chinese police officer in uniform so I was really out of place. Then I was assigned to Chinatown, and doing undercover work on illegal gambling; but everyone knew me in Chinatown, they wouldn't let me into the gambling parlors. Besides there was always the possibility of having to run into my own relatives. I was later reassigned to work on Asian organized crime during the heyday of the Asian gangs in New York.

There was a diversity problem. Asians were not considered a minority, and yet there were few Asian officers in law enforcement. With 7 other police officers and 8 new recruits, we formed the Jade Society of police officers in 1979. We fought and won a class action suit to increase the hiring of Asian police officers. Twenty four years later, our numbers grew exponentially.

Accomplishment: One of the first Asian police officers in NYC, Eugene went on to become a Gold Shield detective.

Hon Lee: From combat Marine and CIA officer to Teacher and Healer

Year Born: 1943
Lived at: Bayard Street, Chinatown
Occupation: Acupuncturist and martial arts teacher (former Marine and CIA Operations Officer)
Father's Occupation: Waiter and then restaurant manager; managed the family business Lee & Lee's almond cookie factory
Mother's Occupation: hairdresser
Biography: Hon K. Lee, a retired Lieutenant Colonel in the United States Marine Corps Reserves, was an artillery forward observer and platoon commander in Vietnam. After leaving active duty, he became a CIA operations officer, serving undercover in seven field assignments and in three of the Agency's four directorates. Studying Chinese medicine after a 30 year CIA career, he is now a nationally certified and board licensed acupuncturist. When not practicing medicine, Lee practices martial arts, having co-founded a school that teaches *kung fu, taijiquan and qigong.* He's married, has two daughters, and lives in Northern Virginia.

Unique experience: Chronicled in his memoir *Paths Less Travelled Of A Scholar Warrior (Spy) Teacher Healer By Hon K. Lee* (2014), North Charleston, SC: CreateSpace Independent Publishing Platform.

Hon K. Lee, a scrawny boy from a Chinese immigrant family living in NYC Chinatown, gets bullied so often he yearns to be like the kung fu heroes he sees in the movies. He becomes a marine to prove himself, but the horrors of war make him wonder what it would take to achieve peace. He joins the CIA, only to see his career threatened in an ordeal that makes him reevaluate his life purpose, leading him to chase his dream to study

Chinese medicine. Along the way, he apprentices with top martial arts masters, and opens a school to pass on what he's learned. In this straightforward, often humorous memoir Lee narrates his adventures from the streets of Chinatown to the battlefields of Vietnam; from the classrooms of the National War College to the corridors of CIA headquarters; and from the kung fu studios of Hong Kong to the acupuncture clinics of Shanghai. While his journey seems to take divergence paths, those familiar with stories about the knights of ancient China will recognize he's travelling a singular path -- a four-fold one of Scholar Warrior Teacher Healer, with Spy thrown in.

Jean Lau Chin: One of the first Asian psychologists to be licensed in the U.S.

Descriptive Quote: Achieved the *Impossible Dream* from my initial hopes simply to graduate from high school and to become a clerk typist.

Year Born: 1944

Lived at: Brooklyn, NY

Occupation: Psychologist and Professor

Father's Occupation: Laundry

Mother's Occupation: Laundry and Seamstress

Accomplishment:.

For her abiding interest, vision and career-long commitment to promoting scholarship on the topic of women and leadership, and For her lifelong devotion to multiculturalism—Quote from one of two presidential citations from the American Psychological Association, Jean Lau Chin has received many awards for her work in psychology.

Biography: Born of Chinese immigrant parents in Bedford Stuyvesant Brooklyn, one of the poorest areas of New York City fraught with gangs, I went on for her doctorate in psychology from Columbia University. Her parents were laundry owners, but instilled the Chinese values of education, personal sacrifice, maintaining harmony, modesty, and hard work. My parents' grade school education led them to feel that a high school diploma was an accomplishment and an endpoint, especially for women; hence, it was to their chagrin for them to see me "do things I never even dreamed of" according to my mother .

In a second presidential citation by American Psychological Association president in 2013, the following inscription was made: "Dr. Chin has had a distinguished career as an educator, administrator, practitioner, leader, scholar, and advocate/policy developer for more than 35 years. She is the "first" in many areas: one of the first Chinese American psychologists in the U.S., the first to be licensed in Massachusetts in 1973, the first psychologist to run the mental health clinic and community health center in Massachusetts, and the first Asian dean at two universities. Her leadership record exemplifies her commitment, as well as the quality of her skills, across the domains of multicultural and feminist psychology. Her work embodies the synthesis of scholarship with advocacy and policy development to improve the lives of people of color, women, LGBT persons, and people living in poverty. Although small in stature, Dr. Chin is a giant in or profession and a powerful voice for diversity and social justice."

Chester Chin: I was one of few Cantonese Chinese Americans graduating from medical school in 1965

Lived: Bronx
Occupation: Orthopedic Surgeon
Father's Occupation: Shirt Pressing Business
Mother's Occupation: Laundry owner born in Boston in 1918
Now living in: New Jersey
Accomplishments: Chester Chin grew up in the Bronx with parents in the laundry and shirt pressing business. He had a long and successful career as an orthopedic surgeon. He was one of the early Cantonese Chinese MDs graduating from medical school in 1965. He went to New York University-University Heights as an undergraduate and received his MD from the SUNY-Downstate Medical Center where he was one of three Chinese Americans in an entering class of 180. His professional orthopedic career was in San Francisco, California where he was an attending physician at six hospitals including the Chinese Hospital located in San Francisco's Chinatown.

Fond memories: My 3 siblings and I would travel from the Bronx to attend Chinese School on weekdays and on Saturday mornings. My brother Peter and I looked forward to Saturday classes because after school, we would play softball with our friends from Chinatown. It was important for us to connect with our heritage, culture and language. Both in drum corp and in Chinese School, many lifelong friendships were formed.

One of Few Chinese: When I went to California in 1971 to practice medicine, I was only one of three Chinese orthopedic surgeons in the area. Living in Hillsborough, CA, we were only one of three Chinese families at the time. When my oldest daughter started elementary school, she was one of two Asians in her public school. Since then, the Asian population in California has grown, and now makes up 15% of the total population. San Francisco is even higher with Asians today making up 35% of the population; Chinese Americans as a group makes up 21%.

Richard Wong: One of two Asians in New York University Law School; you couldn't get a job unless you opened your own practice.

Year Born: 1935
Lived at 36 Mott Street, Chinatown
Mother's Occupation: born in the U.S.; later worked for the Bank of China
Father's Occupation: came at age five from Sun Wei (near Toisan, China.; drove a delivery truck at my grandfather's grocery store, Kung Jung, on 20 Pell Street, which was uncommon because few Chinese Americans had driver's licenses at the time.

Biography: Richard Wong became one of the earliest Chinese Americans to practice law in New York, specializing in immigration law. He was appointed by Governor Hugh Carey to the New York State Human Rights Appeals Board in 1976, and taught at St. John University School of Law as Adjunct Professor of Law in 1980. Before becoming a lawyer, he was an engineer.

Education was always very important in the family. My two grandfathers, in the late 1800s, were both able to read and write fluently in Chinese. In those days very few people were able to do that. Most people had to come illegally as paper sons and laborers because of the anti-Chinese Exclusion Acts. . Because of their education, my maternal grandfather was able to come into this country as a merchant, and bring my maternal grandmother here in 1908. I was the first grandson to finish college.

I went to Wah Keuh Chinese School after American school, which is what most of the kids did. I didn't get good at Chinese though. I learned how to cheat or get through without learning. I got hit with a ruler a lot at Chinese School. When I got home, my grandfather would see the red on my hands and give me another couple of swats because he saw I was bad. Hitting was permissible then. The teacher who flunked me out of Chinese

School gave me an honorary degree 20 years later when I became a lawyer; this degree was more meaningful than my juris doctor because it was the hardest to get."

We lived in a cocoon and were pretty well protected in Chinatown. The people who ran the stores knew all the kids in the neighborhood. If they saw we were bad they reported us to our parents.

My American Public School was about three-quarters Chinese, and one-quarter Italian. After eighth grade, we crossed Canal Street, left Chinatown and went to school in Little Italy. We had to go to school in a group for self-protection. If I was late and missed the group, I would run to school and run home to avoid getting beat up. But then some of the Italian kids got to know some of the Chinese kids and stuck up for us.

I went to Stuyvesant High School, and was very good at math and science, bad at English, history, and language, which was true of most Chinese kids. That's why I decided to go to engineering school. After high school, I went to Polytechnic Rensselaer for college, and became a mechanical engineer in 1956. After a stint in the Navy, I got bored of Engineering, and the discrimination. I went to Law School in 1966, where there were only two Asians at New York University. But then, as an Asian American, you couldn't get a job unless you opened your own practice.

My law professor Judge Irving Younger got elected as Judge of the Civil Court, and offered me the job of law secretary. It was unusual then because law clerks were usually picked by the local political (Democratic or Republican) club. This enabled me to start my law practice in Chinatown—at a time when there were only four or five Chinese American practicing lawyers in the New York area. I partnered with Benjamin Gim, a nationally known immigration lawyer. I was later appointed to the New York State Human Rights Appeals Board by Governor Hugh Carey in 1976. In  1980, I became adjunct professor at St. John's Law School in Queens. I was appointed as a trustee to Beth Israel Medical Center (the only Asian American on the board to this day). I retired from the practice of law in 1985.

Quote: My advice is "make friends, never make enemies, because enemies never forget while friends sometimes forget." My philosophy is that I believe in giving, and giving back to the community. Whatever you give always comes back in double.

Ben Tomm: God bless my father! I could have been a

farmer instead of an architect

Lived at: Eldridge St, Lower East Side
Now living in: New Jersey

Occupation: Architect

Memorable Experience: My father came into the U.S. from Canada into Montana. He was very liberal; he came to NY and became an American citizen. He went back to China to marry his sweetheart from China. The Sino-Japanese war broke out, and my mother and sister were killed by the Japanese; I was the only survivor. My father was a GI at the time fighting the Japanese in China. He didn't know anything about my mother until he came back to US. When he found out, he felt obligated to come back to China to get his only son, me; that was 1948. "God bless my father; he could have left me there and I would have been a farmer instead of an architect."

I went to Transfiguration Chinese School, made very good friends with students at Wah Keuh Chinese School. I have good memories of the comradery in 40s 50s and 60s. Chinatown was like a close family; we learned from each other, did sports and social activities together. We've maintained a 60 year relationship. I still went back to Wing Wor Lung grocery store on Bayard and Mott Street even after my father passed to buy my fish, meat, and groceries; the service was impeccable; the food was fresh; I'm sorry we lost it.

Tom Low: Entrepreneur with a mission

Lived in: Ridgewood, Queens
Now living in: New Jersey
Occupation: Founder of Lee and Low Books
Father's Occupation: Restaurant owner
Biography: I did not live in Chinatown. I grew up outside of Chinatown in a predominantly German and Italian neighborhood. "I developed my resilience. I got along and played sports. There was always prejudice since we were the only Chinese family in Ridgewood, Queens. I learned to develop a tough skin, to look beyond. I made a lot of friends growing up and that caused me to be a stronger person".

We'd come in to Chinatown for dim sum on Monday with my three sisters, brother, mother and father. I have fond memories of tea at Lee's. As I got bigger, I started to come for social activities and met my wife Valentine in 1969; we're married 29 years.

Accomplishment: Tom is an entrepreneur and founded Low & Low Books in 1991, one of the few minority-owned publishing companies in the United States. His sons now run the business. From the website: Lee & Low is also a throwback to what many publishers used to be: independent, generational businesses in which the people running the company have a personal stake in its success. What does it mean to be an independent publisher? It means we make our own decisions and publish what we want. It means we control the quality of our books and keep books in print for a long time so they have a chance to find their audience. It means we have the freedom to pursue our mission of increasing the number of diverse books available to children.

Our story began with a simple mission: to publish contemporary diverse stories that *all* children could enjoy. We decided to steer clear of folktales since they tended to be  about people who lived a long time ago. In contrast, we wanted our books to emphasize the richness of today's cultures. We also avoided talking animal stories since there was nothing new we could bring to this genre.

11: AND WE DID IT IN ONE GENERATION!

This era of the 1940s to 1960s was idyllic but challenging. Although we faced discrimination and many grew up with limited means, the bonds and friendships, community and belongingness led many on to productive lives as American citizens and professional careers outside of the laundries and restaurants. It ended with the Civil Rights movement of the 1960s as Chinatown was also transformed by the notorious rivalry of tongs and gang wars of the late 1960s and 1970s. This changed the image of Chinese Americans, and ushered in a new era with immigration of urban Cantonese Chinese from Hong Kong, waves from Taiwan and other Asian countries, followed by the Fukianese from other rural areas of mainland China who dominate Chinatown today.

We end this book with bios of several Chinese Americans who deserve recognition because of their work and passion to capture the Asian American experience--**Corky Lee** for his passionate photo justice photography which capture images about Asian America, and does his part in rectifying the omissions in history about Asian Americans, and **Gilroy Chow,** who worked on the Apollo Space Shuttle Mission as an engineer and helps to commemorate the oral history of Chinese Americans in the Mississippi Delta. Last but not least, **Theodore Ho**, an engineer, who shares his passion and gratefulness for being given the opportunity to be *born free,* and congratulates the Chinese Americans of NYC for their accomplishments. As he exclaims, and *We did it in one generation!*

Corky Lee: A self-taught photographer, and the "undisputed unofficial Asian American Photographer Laureate."

Year Born: 1944
Lived at: Queens, NY

Occupation: Photographer
Father's Occupation: Laundryman
Mother's Occupation: Seamstress

Biography:

This New York-based photographer has been a fixture at Asian American events, gatherings, meetings, conventions and protests since the 1970s, when the idea of "Asian Americans" instead of separate Chinese, Japanese, Vietnamese, Filipino, etc. communities was a new concept. Corky has covered the day-to-day lives of Asian Pacific Americans, and he's been there to capture some historical moments in American history. He took a memorable group shot of Chinese American descendants of 1800s railroad workers who worked on the joining of the Union Pacific and Central Pacific railroads (the first time that the east and west coasts were connected in trade and commerce by a transcontinental railroad)—a re-creation because Chinese Americans were absent in the original historical photo.

Corky received the Dr. Susan Ahn Civil Rights and Social Justice Award from the Asian American Journalist Association in 2009, a group he help to found. For over 30 years, Corky has used his camera to ensure that the faces of Asian Pacific Americans and their experiences be included in American history. His mission has been to document the incredibly diverse Asian American communities ignored by mainstream media. In an interview in AsianWeek Corky commented, "I'd like to think that every time I take my camera out of my bag, it's like drawing a sword to combat indifference, injustice and discrimination, trying to get rid of stereotypes."

Accomplishment: An Award-winning photojournalist Corky Lee has captured Asian America through his lenses for over three decades! His photos are intensely personal and socially conscious; his self-styled photojournalism crosses the divides of different Asian nationalities, and presents a rich picture of AAPIs adjusting and finding their place in America. As a photojournalist imbued with an unyielding passion for community activism, he's challenged stereotypes by offering diverse images from the often invisible and excluded Asian Pacific American communities.

His work, which has been described as "only a small attempt to rectify omissions in our history text books," has appeared in Time magazine, The New York Times, The Village Voice, Associated Press, The Villager and Downtown Express, as well as exhibitions throughout the United States, including Boston, San Francisco, Honolulu and Denver. On college campuses, his photographs have been exhibited at Cornell, Columbia, Harvard, Princeton and John Jay College of Criminal Justice in New York City.

Gilroy Chow: Someone has to tell the story.

Nickname: Gil
Year Born: 1940
Lived at: Queens, NY
Living today in: Mississippi Delta area
Occupation: Engineering manager
Father's Occupation: Owned Chinese restaurant; Executive in Import Export Business located in Empire State Building.
Mother's Occupation: Owned Chinese restaurant

Quote: Gilroy has been instrumental in documenting the Oral History of the Chinese in the Mississippi Delta area. He enjoyed growing up in a large Chinese Family in NYC and moved back to the Mississippi Delta area where Chinese-Americans go back a century or more. Using the ingredients at hand and the techniques passed on for generations, Gilroy says: "What we eat connects us so that we know we are both Chinese and Mississippi Delta folks" as he cooked crayfish Cantonese style in an outdoor wok.

Biography: The best lesson I learned early in life was to treat everyone with dignity and respect. This was true for everyone, regardless of age, race, religion, socioeconomic status or position. My dad instilled in me as a young man that, although I was visually different, I had the same opportunities to develop skills and abilities as everyone else. It was up to me to work diligently to learn and apply them and then make the most of those opportunities. The opportunities we get are a result of relationships, and those relationships largely depend on people treating one another with the dignity and respect they deserve. I believe it was a lesson that he had personally learned as a 12-year-old immigrant from Canton, China, coming to the "Gold Mountain," working many long hours in a grocery store in Mississippi to being the managing partner in an import-export firm operating in the Empire State building in New York. While his formal education ended in the third grade, he still managed to reach a point where he had 25 PhD's working for him through his own initiative and imagination. He told me that you didn't have to know everything, but if you knew enough of who and where to turn for information you can go a long way. His passport name was "J.T. Im." This gave rise to using the business introduction of accomplishing that and more, he took the time to teach me that according everyone with dignity and respect was key to success in life. This is probably truer today than the time I first heard it years ago.

Accomplishment: Gilroy worked on the Apollo Space Shuttle Program between 1966-1973. His work ranged from building mock-ups and prototypes of concepts in Bethpage, N.Y. to installing ground support equipment at the launch pads of Cape Canaveral, Fla.; to training astronauts in simulators in Houston, Texas,

East Meets South at a Delta Table

Chinese-Americans bring the tastes of their ancestors down home.

Figure 1. Joan Nathan. "East Meets South at a Delta Table: Chinese-Americans bring the tastes of their ancestors down home," New York Times. June 4 2003: D1–D 5.

and Merritt Island, Fla.; and then being involved in 11 mission launches and splashdowns. He says, I really can't single out a most interesting moment. For a young engineer just out of Mississippi State University, it was a great adventure to be working on a "man-rated" spacecraft, unique in design, using new and exotic materials and "state of the art" equipment in new and different places. I just thought that was the way it was supposed to be for everyone. Even being surrounded with all of the technology and scientific expertise, looking back, I think the most impressive accomplishment of the Apollo Program was to build and mold a high-achieving team of diverse (geographic and cultural) backgrounds, and then hold that team's efforts at sustained high levels of performance over a long period. Consistently doing myriad tasks for extended periods to achieve mission objectives, being dependent on others, while being a dependable team member. I think of the massive organizational skills that were brought to bear to accomplish the objective "for America ... to send men to the moon by the end of this decade, and return them safely to earth." Just being a part of the team that achieve the goal that was set before us was "Simply ... awesome!" (Adapted from: http://www.pressregister.com/article_b6994330-3f58-5207-b732-9f3341aa03a4.html?mode=print 1/5; 12/16/2014 Our Town: Gilroy Chow - Clarksdale Press Register: Home)

Theodore Ho: And we did it in one generation!

Quote: Grateful for my parent's long journey to America and giving me the opportunity to be born free. We established ourselves, *and We did it in one generation!*
Nickname: Ted
Year Born: 1933
Lived at: 37 Mott Street and 82 Bayard Street, Chinatown
Occupation: Engineer
Father's Occupation: Owned Chinese restaurant
Mother's Occupation: Housewife
Family business: Mee Heung Noodle Company

Biography: My father ended up in Liverpool England before coming to the US. My mother died when I was six. We had to cross Canal St to go to junior high; nowadays, they call it bullying. Since I wear glasses, I had several pairs broken; I had to make it home across Canal Street before they came at us. When we went to buy our first house, the neighbors petitioned in an attempt to prevent us from buying a house in the neighborhood because we were Chinese.

Fondest Memory: All those in my generation spoke Cantonese first, English was actually first taught to me by my kindergarten teacher. I always felt safe in Chinatown, everyone knew everyone, and all my seniors were Aunt or Uncle something. Our parents wanted us to be more than they were. They wanted us to be educated so that we could excel and be all that we could be. I believe, we within that generation fulfilled their hopes for us. My fondest memory in Chinatown was the feeling of security and togetherness. Our little secured hamlet kept us insulated from the ugliness of prejudice.

Growing Experience and resiliency of stress: Living in the cocoon safety of Chinatown did not prepare me for the overt prejudice beyond our walls. Attending PS 130 was a nightmare for us ABCs (American Born Chinese). Every day had its violence after school....fighting for our dignity and self-esteem. We were totally unprepared for the baiting and beatings that ensued. Ultimately you toughen up and get ready for the day ending fight with bullies. It was an eye opener...bullies get their way when you show fear. Fighting back made them think twice. Perhaps these early challenges helped prepare me for greater tests in life.

I think we should take pride in our accomplishments. We should be mindful that our parents came here illegally, but *in one generation,* many of us have had a very good education. Many of us came out of Chinatown. **Daniel Lee** and I worked together at Grumman some 30 years ago and just reconnected because of this Oral History project. He wrote very proudly about our accomplishments—Our parents came because they had to come, but what they did was to give us an opportunity. We  have taken that opportunity, *and In one generation, We have established ourselves.*

INDEX OF NAMES

Last Name	First Name	Page
Chan	Ann	31
Chan	Elsie	68
Chan	Joseph	75
Cheu	Lillian	81
Chin	Ivan	33
Chin	Leilani	34
Chin	Helen	35
Chin	John	47
Chin	Helen	68
Chin	Jean Marie	68
Chin	Donald	73
Chin	Dottie	89
Chin	Ed	92
Chin	Marion	100
Chin	Jean Lau	107
Chin	Chester	108
Chiu	Debra (Gong)	48
Chow	Pearl	75
Chow	Gilroy	115
Chu	Elaine	47
Chu	Richard	54
Chu	Lai	98
Chung Davis	Margie	93
Dilger	Louise Leong	51
Gong	Park	92
Ho	Lily	87
Ho	Theodore	117
Hum	Henry	92

Kwong	Irene	34
Kwong	George	45
Lai-Ong	Warner	39
Lau	Willie	50
Lau	Larry	74
Lee	William	31
Lee	Sandra K.	35
Lee	Clifford	36
Lee	Daniel	60
Lee	Anna	77
Lee	Rosemary	79
Lee	John	84
Lee	Ray	89
Lee	Baayork	104
Lee	Eugene	105
Lee	Hon	106
Lee	Corky	114
Leung	Lucy	43
Low	Tom	111
Lui	Harold	95
Lui	Ronald	95
Mok	John	30
Moy	Gingee	67
Moy	Calvin	75
Moy	Daniel	81
Moy	James Y.K.	87
Moy	Daniel K.	91
Ong Shu	Anna	43
Sham	Mary	63
Tom	Valerie	46
Tomm	Ben	111
Wong	Richard	109
Woo	Gene	66
Woo	Harry	94
Yee	Gloria	36

ABOUT THE AUTHORS

Jean Lau Chin, Ed.D., ABPP is a psychologist and Professor at Adelphi University in New York. She has held senior management positions as academic Dean at two universities, Executive Director of a community health center, and Director of a mental health clinic. Currently, her work on leadership, diversity, and women's issues has included designation as a Senior Fulbright Specialist, and author of 12 books, and numerous publications. She has served in many leadership positions on national, state and local boards promoting national policy on mental health, substance abuse, access to care, cultural competence, Asian American and women's issues. She was the first Asian American to be licensed as a psychologist in Massachusetts. She grew up in New York City's Chinatown during the 1940s-1960s, and has been a major contributor to the New York City Chinatown Oral History Project.

Daniel Lee (Danny) is an Electronic Engineer, ME, MBA, PE. He was in Corporate Management at Aerospace and Electronic Warfare Corporations. He was also Adjunct Professor in Mathematics & Engineering Management. He is now retired. He serves on various boards, does periodic consulting, is a volunteer and legislative advocate for the Disability Community. His recreational passions include: Skiing, Sailing, and Dancing. He is married to Sharon (Camp) and lives in Nashua, New Hampshire; he feel blessed with a lovely, beautiful wife, three wonderful outstanding children, and six gorgeous grandchildren. He grew up in NYC Chinatown, offers a note of "love and appreciation to my Mom and Dad for their strength and resiliency in teaching us, through everyday life examples of our Chinese family values and the importance of education. Our many church groups in Chinatown who provided the vital teachings and lessons to lead a good Christian life."

www.ingramcontent.com/pod-product-compliance
Lightning Source LLC
Chambersburg PA
CBHW060411290526
45791CB00002B/707